Your Child From Six To Twelve

By Marion L. Faegre

www.sunvillagepublications.com

Your Child From Six To Twelve
By Marion L. Faegre

Copyright © 2010

www.sunvillagepublications.com

Cover design by www.WebCopyAlchemy.com

Foreword

Katherine B. Oettinger, Chief, Children's Bureau, U. S. Department of Health, Education, and Welfare, in the Foreword to the latest edition of "Your Child from Six to Twelve," wrote:

"There are many more things that we don't know then we do know about children. This is hard on us parents, because instead of being given directions about how to 'get' our children to do this or that, or being told at what ages we can expect certain developments, we have to work more or less in the dark. How pleasant it would be if we had definite rules as to how to develop to the full our children's inborn abilities! And yet perhaps one of the most intriguing things about being a parent is the mystery and unpredictability surrounding these unique beings entrusted to our care for a few years. Maybe we are just as happy, and they a lot more so, because we don't have any magic formula by which to direct their lives.

"Yet there are many kinds of knowledge that would help us out enormously when it comes to the everyday problems of family life. If only we knew how to get children to *want* to do the things we feel pretty sure they'll profit by learning, such as keeping their rooms neat, and doing their home work on time!

"Such methods of influencing behavior will have to wait until we know a great deal more than we do now — about ourselves as well as about children. Man has uncovered more of the secrets of the universe than he has of the secret doings of the human heart and mind; it's much harder to delve into the ways people act and think and feel than it is even to find out what's going on among the stars.

"But thoughtful parents try honestly to put to use what knowledge we now have. We can add to what we know by close observation of our children, and so let them inform us much about their needs and what can be expected of them. Each time we learn this way we take a step forward along the road to better parenthood.

"This book was written by Mrs. Marion L. Faegre, under the direction of Dr. Katherine Bain, Director of the Division of Research in Child Development. Helpful suggestions were also received from other members of the Children's Bureau staff. Sincere thanks are due to the members of our Pediatric Advisory Committee, and to the professional persons and parents who also reviewed the manuscript."

Contents

Editors' Foreword

Your Child From Six to Twelve is the fourth in the Child Care series, written to help you to be more confident and intelligent parents. *Prenatal Care,* the first in the series, was designed to see you safely through pregnancy and the birth of your baby. *Infant Care* helped you take care of your new baby through his first year. *Your Child from One to Six* carried on from your child's first birthday.

This book is an up-to-date, informative, reliable and authoritative guide for parents of children in the formative years of six to twelve. It was written under the direction of the Division of Research in Child Development of the Children's Bureau of the United States government, and reviewed by its Pediatric Advisory Committee and other professional persons trained in child development.

While your children were very little things happened around your house because you willed them to. Your youngsters were completely dependent on you for their well-being and companionship. Their daily routines were determined by you.

But as they reach school age and continue to blossom out as definite personalities, you will find that they have minds of their own. Their abilities, likes and dislikes, dispositions, and dreams make them unlike any other children you know. Their minds are opened to the influences of other adults. Their secret hearts are torn or warmed by the companionship of other children of their own age.

There can be no set, fixed book of rules for guiding, helping to develop, and making completely happy children of early school years. Each child is a special person who requires special care. But those who have had wide experience in observing, teaching, and helping to develop the possibilities of children of this age group can give parents the benefit of their advice.

That is what this book purports to do. It will tell you what you can expect as your child progresses from one growth adventure to the next. It will guide you in handling what might seem to be problems. It will help you avoid some of the pitfalls that might have unhappy results. It will take some of the surprise, and disconcerting anxiety out of your own reactions to your child's behavior.

We hope this book will help you to be wiser, more comfortable, and more self-confident as you continue your job of rearing and training the constantly changing younger members of your family.

I

What 6- to 12-year-olds are

To thoughtful parents, the school-age period of children's development is even more interesting than the appealing years of early childhood. Boys and girls are trying out their own abilities and interests, and are gaining in self-confidence and self-reliance. While they still need and count on the friendly care and backing of their parents and others in the family, they manage more and more of their own affairs. The feeling that the loyalty and service they give their family is appreciated is highly enjoyable to them.

During this period, while a child's personality is becoming increasingly complex, it becomes more of a challenge to understand him. His growing independence and ability to think and reason for himself are sometimes disconcerting. It upsets our superiority just a bit when our children begin to question our opinions, and to have very definite ideas of their own.

"I'm quite as big for me," said he, "as you are big for you."

1

This is really what scares many an adult off. While a child is very young and also very ignorant we older people feel secure in our bigness and power. We feel important in contrast to the child's smallness and helplessness. We enjoy his naive way of looking at life because we can say to ourselves, "Oh, we know all about that!" But as children grow out of complete dependence, they begin to think and reason for themselves.

We tend to be less observant of school-age children because their development is far less spectacular, in many ways, than that of the young child. Physical growth has slowed down greatly. Mental growth goes on so quietly we take it for granted. While a child is learning to talk everything he says is novel and arresting. Once he gets into middle childhood his ability to understand things and to express himself has progressed so much that what he says no longer seems so remarkable. His reasoning is much better; he no longer argues amusingly that butter is made from butterflies because the two words sound alike; he stops believing that trees make the wind blow.

Nor is his health a cause for quite such vigilance as earlier. Once a child has passed through the preschool years, the time of greatest danger from childhood diseases, his parents become a little less watchful and anxious. He can take care of himself much of the time; they no longer feel worried every minute he's out of their sight.

CHILDREN ARE SELF-STARTERS

In short, he is on the way to becoming a self-contained, self-directing, self-motivated person. Still close to his parents, still appreciating attention, love, and sympathy, he is striking out for himself, making friends, showing individual tastes, exploring many fields—a lively, eager, able, light-hearted, and often maddening creature. He is tremendously interested in the things and life about him. As he approaches the teens he will become interested in himself, but now his thoughts are mostly turned outwards toward the practical, material world.

Does this sound as if all children are alike? Of course they're not. They're as different and varied and surprising in their individuality as in their looks but there are ideas, feelings, ways of acting and looking at things which they all go through at certain stages in their growth.

BODILY SKILLS ARE ADDED FAST

Once a child has acquired good control over his body, he has a great deal of energy to expend on learning skills and adding to all manner of abilities that were only partially perfected before.

Little girls of 6 to 10, for example, delight in hop-scotch and jacks, which call for more precise muscular adjustment than the large-muscle activities of their early childhood. The intricate rhythm of skipping rope, fancy stunts on a bicycle or on roller-skates all involve bodily control that was not possible at 4 or 5. Learning to whistle, to turn handsprings, to balance a pole on the open hand, to bounce a ball in time to a special pattern of bodily movements—all these kinds of skills delight the boys and girls who are coming to have more and more control over their muscles. Learning to write requires very exact adjustments and coordination between hand and eye. (Remember your struggles not to get the tail of the "y" too far below the line, and to keep the "e's" from looking like Ts"?) Increasing ability to use the fingers makes later childhood a time in which such things as playing a musical instrument or typing should be getting under way if they are to become highly developed.

Children can't get enough of games that emphasize physical alertness. Chasing, climbing, dodging are a never-ending joy. Swinging, on a proper swing if that's all that's handy, better on a grapevine discovered in the woods, frees them from being earth-bound clods. Tag, run-sheep-run, "cops and robbers"—anything in which there's the thrill and excitement of avoiding capture appeals to the "wild Indian" stage of the early school years.

NATURE'S DOOR IS WIDE OPEN

Caves and tree-houses, dams and pools, fires to roast potatoes in, trees to climb and swamps to explore—nature's resources seem made to be exploited by children. Imagination is at a high peak; the early school-age child becomes what he has read about or heard of or listened to. He re-creates the life about him; boys build houses, girls set up housekeeping in them.

Animals are children's close kin. Children know

". . . how to handle puppies, with propitiatory pats For mother dogs, and little acts of courtesy to cats'

A boy and his dog are attached to each other by invisible, unbreakable ties. The tenderness with which an injured bird or a motherless lamb is cared for shows us what wonderfully responsive creatures our children are. They may not have as good a chance later to learn

"How the tortoise bears his shell, How the
woodchuck digs his cell, And the
ground-mole sinks his well";

Children's joy in the world of nature is matched by their delight in putting their hands to work.

The school-age child constructs things with initiative and fervor. Carts, kites, airplanes, boats are undertaken with varying degrees of success according to the skill present at different ages and individual cleverness in the use of the hands. Girls cut out paper dolls by the dozen, make dresses for them by the score. Weaving, knot-tying, carving, all have their devotees.

Not only is this when children prove and improve their physical skill, it is a time for trying out everything under the sun. Eight- or nine-year-olds have a greater variety of play interests than children of any age. Later on, after a child has explored a great many possibilities it becomes necessary to spend more time on well-liked ones if he is to become good at them. But now—now there's time for everything.

THEIR MOTTO: TRY ANYTHING ONCE

Experimentation leads children everywhere. It urges them into using every one of their senses. They discover the sweet taste of the growing ends of grass blades, and sample pungent, tangy pine needles. They make leaves squawk, tear apart paper-thin birch-bark layers. They rub the leaves of mint and sniff its fragrance and say "phew!" to the "cow-pie" they almost stepped in.

They burrow into the haystack, climb on top and come hurtling down with dust in their hair. They run, panting, after the fire engine, hoping the fire will be a big one. When the plumber comes to the house, they're right under foot, watching. And when a street is being paved, every operation is followed by fascinated eyes. They can't wait for it to come time to go barefoot, when they can "squdge" mud between their toes, or feel

THE CHÍID BETWEEN 6 AND 7

Physical growth and skills. Has six or seven wrist bones. Has one or two permanent teeth. "Knock-knees" of preschool period have disappeared. Very active; sitting still is an effort; wriggling especially noticeable at table. Absorbed in running, jumping, chasing, and dodging games. Enjoys any sort of wheel toy. Likes to bathe self, with help on ears, neck, and back. Can dress self without help, even to tying shoe laces, but is inclined to dawdle.

Social progress. Thoroughly enjoys group play, but groups tend to be small. Boys and girls play together. Boys begin to wrestle, have fist fights, often with good friends; must prove their masculinity. Parties greatly in favor, but behavior is unlikely to be decorous. Able to use telephone competently. Teacher's opinions and ideas very important. Rapid alternation between "good" and "bad" behavior.

Intellectual growth and activities. Commonly uses upward of 2,500 words. Delights in imaginative dramatic play; may carry on long conversations with imaginary person after going to bed. May believe radio characters are real. Knows comparative value of the common coins. Knows own address, parents' names, how to cross street. From now up to the teens adventure programs on television and radio much liked. Name-calling, vulgar talk common. Belief in Santa Claus may be fading. Knows number combinations making up to 10. The beginning steps in learning to read greatly delight the child.

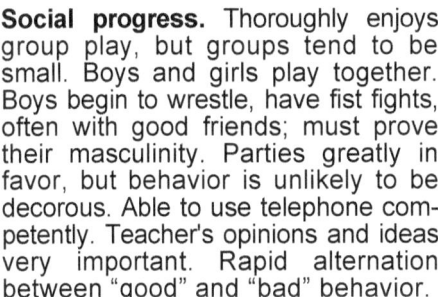

the cold tingle of dew-wet grass. They like to bite and suck and chew on anything, from slippery elm to bubble gum and pencils.

A rain-filled gutter cries out to be stepped in, rubbers or no rubbers. Soap is something to work up a lather with, rather than something to get clean with.

They love the rites and rhymes and tricks that are handed down perennially by older children, like "wire, brier, limber lock" and "Adam and Eve and pinch-me." They like to believe that without question they'll get their wish on the "first star."

Guessing games, riddles, conundrums and jokes all have their day. Code language is rattled off by two 9-year-olds as fast as they can talk. Charades are a gold mine of fun. Dressed up in mother's cast-off dresses and high-heeled shoes, little girls pay very formal calls, or have baby parades with their doll carriages. Table games consume lots of time; although there's a painful period until children understand that someone must be the loser. Hard to take at first, this is an important kind of learning, and paves the way for team play later. Sending away for samples, saving box tops or coupons, making collections of anything and everything, and jealously hoarding these nondescript treasures; following the iceman for pieces of ice to suck; haunting the back premises of grocery stores in the hope of getting boxes to build with; pouncing on the evening paper so as not to lose a minute in looking at the funnies—these are almost as characteristic of our 6- to 12-ers as eating is.

"BED AND BOARD"

Sleep is something made for babies or aged parents, a terrible waste of time for those whose days are far too short to get everything in. Energetic children hate to be inactive, unless they've an absorbing book, a piece of string to play cat's cradle with, or some other way to occupy their fingers.

Sleeping may be a bore, but eating is a joy forever. Preferably, children think, eating should be done in a hurry. If food tastes extra good, why, naturally it should be gobbled; if it's something you don't like but have to eat—gulp it down fast, after you've left it on your plate till the very last. And as for the folly of eating at set times—who ever invented such nonsense? Meals are all very well, but how are children going to last between them, when they're tearing all over the neighborhood,

THE CHILD BETWEEN 7 AND 8

Physical growth and skills. Adds from 3 to 5 pounds weight yearly. Slow, regular growth in height. "Nervous habits" like nail-biting, tongue-sucking, scratching, pulling at ear common, but show no increase from 6 to 12; more frequent in girls than in boys. Less impulsive and boisterous in actions than at 6. Jumping rope, hop-scotch, and jacks popular with girls.

Social progress. Recognition of property rights sketchy. Competition in school, at play, begins to be present. From now on becomes more interested in dressing and acting like his friends. Choice of friends uninfluenced by social or economic status. Demands of the environment make learning to use money desirable. When angry at parents may toy with idea he is not their child. Awareness of differences between his home and those of others increasing.

Intellectual growth and activities. Child's ability to make things is not up to his ideas of what he would like to do. Can count by l's, 2's, 5's, and 10's. Can grasp the basic ideas of addition and subtraction. Can tel! time; sometimes knows what month it is. Ability to run errands, make purchases, take responsibility generally on the increase from now on. Often argues about what he is expected to do. Curiosity about differences between the sexes and how babies come indicates increasing interest in reality, and suggests importance of giving truthful information.

doing important things like riding bicycles, climbing trees, or planning a show? A 10-year-old is absolutely empty, caved in, after school.

The 6- to 12-year old has quite a different attitude toward clothes than he did when younger. He is much more conscious of what other children wear, and wants to look like them. To be different is as hard on a child of this age as it is on a man who feels too short or a woman who thinks she is too fat. Shoes, caps, dresses, or hair-do's unlike those worn by most children can cause acute humiliation.

As for older and younger children in the same family—what a gulf exists between them at school and at play! "We don't want you tagging along! Scram!" is the attitude of the older ones who like to think of themselves as far more grown up than their little sisters and brothers.

But older brothers and sisters often display a tenderly protective care over little ones that is beautiful to see. It gives us intimations of their boundless possibilities for consideration and gentleness, which will be developed to the full when they themselves are parents.

Along about 9 or 10, boys begin to be intolerant of girls, and girls to turn up their noses at boys. Oh, each sex is all right when it comes to games that need a number of players. But girls are scary things, say the boys, who like to make them shriek by holding dead mice under their noses, or grabbing their ankles under water. And boys are rough, and careless, according to girls. Do they ever comb their hair? But underneath this exaggerated contempt for each other lurks an attraction that before very many years will become strong.

Brothers and sisters are allies one minute, scrappy as alley cats the next. There are times when each seems to get delight out of tormenting the other: Ned gets Polly at his mercy and tickles her. She in turn tattles on him in a most disagreeable way. But let an outsider pick on one or the other and right away, Ned or Polly is up in arms defending the other.

At this stage either one of them is probably quite willing to skip the daily bath in order to have more time to play. Or, they both claim the bathroom at the same time when they *do* decide to bathe!

2

How family life is different today

Why is it considered more of a problem to raise children nowadays than it used to be? Many parents are puzzled to know why there is so much spoken and written about the bringing up of children. "Our parents raised us without so much fuss over whether they were doing everything just right. Why is it necessary all of a sudden to make such a to-do about being parents?"

It's a very natural question. For the changes that have made raising a family a different matter from what it was only relatively few years back came about gradually. We accept them so matter-of-factly that we don't realize our children are living in another world from that in which we grew up—not to mention the unclimbable walls separating their world from the world of their grandparents. If parents have more problems now it's partly because they are so much more aware of children's needs and possibilities, but are confused as to how to go about meeting the needs and providing for the expansion of the possibilities.

LIVING CONDITIONS ARE CHANGING

For one thing, fewer people live in the country. Bringing up children in town on a small lot or in a city apartment means opportunities for activity are cut down; the freedom that rural children enjoy is missing. Dammed up energy must find a way out; the town child's "fun" may easily result in his getting into mischief, because his acts may infringe on the peace and quiet and property of close-up neighbors. The city boy and girl can't even sing and whistle and shout as much as their country cousins. In an apartment, they may have to change to slippers the minute they come inside, so that their clatter won't annoy the family below.

FAMILIES ARE SMALLER

Another new problem that parents face nowadays is the likelihood that their child may not have as many brothers and sisters as they had. The proportion of people who have no children has risen so sharply that there may be few children to play with in a given neighborhood. In 1910, less than 10 percent of families had no children, while in 1940, the proportion bad risen to over 15 percent. More children nowadays have only one or two brothers and sisters, and thus grow up in a very different atmosphere from that surrounding the child who is one of several, and to whom it would seem unnatural to have so much parental attention as many children get today.

INVENTIONS ALTER FAMILY LIFE

Still another change that makes parents' teaching of their children different from what they were taught in childhood is the great number of inventions that lessen household toil. Washing machines (or laundries that do the whole job away from home), vacuum cleaners, oil burners, tractors, electric refrigerators and other inventions have decreased the number of jobs that children have to help with. Not so many years ago it took three people to do the cleaning that one person can now do alone. No longer do so many children have to beat rugs, bring in ice and carry out ashes. For every child who shovels snow there may be another whose apartment house janitor does it for him. The baker sometimes calls with bread, even in the country.

THE CHILD BETWEEN 8 AND 9

Physical growth and skills. Ten or eleven permanent teeth. Growing interest in games requiring coordination of small muscles (hitting moving target, shooting marbles, catching with one hand, etc.). Ability to write progressing, but fine muscle work is still difficult and taxing. Can swim well, if there has been opportunity for learning. Can bicycle and roller skate expertly. Bathes self, but sketchily.

Social progress. Evidence of modesty may be increasing, due probably to social pressures. Group projects become absorbing, but child is not yet entirely capable of team play. Recognition of property rights well established if training has been sound. Manners often better away from home than at home. Is becoming more selective in choice of friends. Dolls and paper-doll play mimics family life.

Intellectual growth and activities. Begins to be interested in what happened in the distant past (likes to make Indian costumes, utensils, etc.). Fairy tales are great favorites with both boys and girls. Can tell day of month and year. Can make change for small amounts. Begins to read the funnies, a favorite occupation from now on. Radio and television are main interests, but begins to be skeptical of "realness" of programs. Sense of humor marked, especially in bright children. Experience has opened the door to interest in the world at large. Far-off places, ways of communication now have real meaning.

Children whose families haven't conveniences and luxuries are exposed to those whose life is more comfortable, and so *their* lives are affected by their knowledge of what they are missing.

In cities, a problem often comes up when a mother and father try to give their youngsters the benefit of the work around the house that was a natural part of their own young life, and that they feel pretty sure was a good part. What can take the place of that learning? To be sure there are still meals to get, dishes to wash, and errands to run. But where before the necessity for all hands to pitch in was plain to be seen, so many things can now be bought or done outside the home that many city children get little practice in cooperative living.

The mother of a little girl who wants a new dress for a special occasion may say, "All right, I'll have time to make one if you keep the house looking neat all week." The child's reply may be "Oh, why don't you buy me a dress, instead?" The advertising she sees seems to make buying easy and "making" unnecessary.

RECREATION MOVES OUTSIDE

Along with the bread-making, laundry, and sewing that have gone out of many homes have gone some of the home-made ways of having fun. As cities grew, commercial amusements sprang up to take advantage of the increasing amount of free time town dwellers had. Movies, roller-skating rinks, bowling alleys, night baseball games, offer thrills to millions of children who, a generation or two back, would have been content with a phonograph, ice skating on the creek, and only an occasional fling at an amusement park or a county fair. In a way, the radio gathers the family together at home, on occasion, and television is another magnet that draws families back into their homes.

Changes in size of family, living conditions, and changes due to labor-saving machines are all external things. And yet they affect people's inner lives, their ways of thinking, feeling, and acting. Life in an apartment or on a rented farm, with frequent moves, means changes in relations with other people: there is less need to care about and be thoughtful of others, when we don't even know our neighbors' names.

Having a movie only a block or so away means that youngsters feel a strong pull to see the films they hear talked about, no matter how pleasant their home life is. Children who live on farms are affected by the spread of commercial amusements, too. How many country boys and girls who leave home to work in cities have been tempted to do so by the life they have seen on the screen?

EARLIER OUTSIDE INFLUENCES

A child now gets out into the stream of things earlier—in fact, the world comes right into our homes, by way of the radio and magazines. The latest song hits, however unsuitable, are on the lips of 6-year-olds. This means that his parents are dealing with a child who is much more "knowing" than they were at his age; who has at least a surface acquaintance with the ways of the world.

So fathers and mothers are up against very different problems, and a wider variety of them than they used to be. Important as it has always been to understand our children, there are pressures on us nowadays that didn't exist earlier. To meet them calls for great skill.

FATHERS SEE LESS OF THEIR CHILDREN

Conditions within homes have changed, too, with changing pressures from outside. Fathers have less time at home; many live farther from their work, and few have their shops or offices in their homes. This means that a great part of child training falls on the mother.

But even mother is not always in the home. A larger and larger percent of women work outside, most of them because they have to, some because they want to provide advantages for their children. How does this affect family life?

When the children in one family are put more upon their own responsibility because their mother works outside, they are not the only ones affected. If Jane's mother lets her go to the movies three times a week, so that she'll not be roaming the neighborhood after school, Mrs. Brown's Sally is going to want to go with Jane, even though *her* mother is at home. Every change that affects *any* family affects our family, too.

THE CHILD BETWEEN 9 AND 10

Physical growth and skills. Slow growth in height. Last wrist bone appears in girls. Teeth straightening, if needed, can be begun. Can care for physical needs like baths,' hair combing, etc. Uses tools increasingly well. Many children at this time and later need more rest and sleep than they get, because constantly "on the go," and interested in so many different kinds of play. Disdainful of danger, but gets into plenty of it.

Social progress. Sex differences in play interests begin to be marked. More different kinds of play engaged in than ever again. Antagonism between sexes noticeable for next several years; longer for boys than girls. "Gang" and club enthusiasm noticeable, with hostility toward other groups; exclusion an important feature of clubs, which are short-lived. Visits alone away from home; may go to camp. Some of spontaneity of relations with adults may be giving place to reticence, even to hostility, shown by having secrets.

Intellectual growth and activities. Can grasp easier multiplication and division facts. Differences in boys' and girls' reading interests begin to be noticeable. Bright children begin to use card indexes at library and read full-length books. Begins to have friends outside immediate neighborhood. Interest in fantasy and make-believe on the decline. Comedians, news broadcasters, drama in general more and more appreciated on radio; boys like programs of greater violence than girls. Interest in how things are made, produced, etc., is increasing. If interest in a special field—science, nature, or mechanics—has developed this may begin to crowd out some other play activities.

THE DEMOCRATIC FAMILY

The problems parents encounter, then, multiply as life becomes more complicated. No one can live apart from the speeded-up and closer-knit world. Whether they like it or not, parents belong to the "one world" of which we can't lose consciousness a minute. Theirs is the privilege of providing a kind of family life that will prepare their children for living in a world where their fate hangs on their being real world citizens.

What kind of family life will encourage this?

The family is a tiny world in itself, in which children receive practice and preparation for wider living. Unless the family life is wholesomely democratic and cooperative, how can children learn the skills that will ready them to take part in a society that can continue only through the combined efforts of all to make it work? The present struggle to find ways of bettering relations among nations may make us blushingly conscious that family relations, too, could stand improvement. We should become more aware of how family life can serve all the individuals it is made up of, and determine to make our family life a fine example of this.

What does democratic family living mean? It means a way of life in which:

Parents care so deeply for each other that they are just as anxious for their partners to gain their wishes as to get what they want for themselves. The needs of all, grown-ups and children, are considered and met just as far as possible. Father and mother and children all have a voice in decisions that concern them, and parents and children alike are serving as, or learning by practice how to be, good community members.

3

What successful parenthood involves

We were people before we were parents. The kind of people we are impresses itself so deeply on our children that the best of efforts don't amount to much if our own personalities get in the way. In other words, we must understand ourselves, our own longings, frustrations, and good points before we can hope to do a bang-up job as parents.

Children will overlook a lot in a mother and father who really love them. They can stand being scolded, or even punished, by a mother who is warmhearted, and enjoys her children. They will thrive better under her care than under that of a patient, outwardly devoted mother who is inwardly cold, selfish, and resentful, or of one who is constantly afraid of doing the wrong thing.

Family jokes are one of the finest means of enabling children to feel comradeship with their parents. Laughter eases strain and apprehension. Even a rebuke, given in a way that causes a child to laugh at himself, contributes to his sense of security since he feels bigger than his mistake. Laughing together provides many of the warmest memories of home life.

It's a good thing parenthood comes fairly early in life. Young people haven't had time to get quite so hard and set in their ways. But each generation reflects the effect of the last on its offspring; we can't get away from that. A parent whose personality is very masterful sometimes overawes his children into socially acceptable behavior. We may not have the faintest idea that we are "dominating"; we may be only unconsciously adopting toward our children ways that were used by our own parents. It seems natural to give orders, to have our opinions respected, to have John and Ann jump when we call. If we were used to the same kind of father- or mother-behavior we may not see that we are making our children afraid to express themselves, and more yielding and submissive than will be good for their relations with other people. We all need to take stock once in a while, and to keep in mind that allowing children to develop into the fine human beings they can become is as important as directing them.

Of course there are mild, gentle submissive parents, too. Their lack of strength may result in their children's acting stubborn and balky when they try to get their way with others as they have with their yielding parents. Ordinarily, these tendencies are somewhat evened up by the fact that children have two parents; they learn to balance their behavior in relation to two different temperaments. Art's father may be easygoing, his mother somewhat dictatorial. The boy adjusts to and is influenced by both. And, luckily, he influences them, too.

DO WE REALLY ACCEPT OUR CHILDREN?

Most important of all to a child's future personality is a feeling of being approved of, accepted, and enjoyed by his parents. Children who grow up in an atmosphere of security have confidence in themselves. They can face both the present and the future without the perplexing doubts that trouble children who don't feel this sureness. How can Barbara feel accepted if her mother constantly laments her daughter's straight hair or her freckles? Won't Leo's belief in himself be less sturdy if his father is impatient over his difficulties with arithmetic?

Children need the assurance of feeling that their parents are proud of them; of knowing that no matter what scrapes they

THE CHILD BETWEEN 10 AND 11

Physical growth and skills. Rapid increase in weight may begin in girls. Has 14 or 16 permanent teeth. Willing to work hard at acquiring physical skills; emphasis is on excellence of performance of physical feats. Interest in hazardous activities points the need for safe places to play. Boys more active and rough in games than girls.

Social progress. Organized and competitive games more and more prominent. Team-work, submission to fixed rules in play now possible. Occasional privacy becomes important; a room of one's own, secret caches for personal property are greatly desired.

Intellectual growth and activities. Ability to plan ahead is increasing. Gathering factual information important, especially among boys. Uses numbers beyond 100 with understanding. Begins to understand and use simple fractions. Able to discuss problems, to see different sides of questions. Interested in other people's ideas. Likes to set up rules and bylaws for clubs. Steadily growing capacity for thought and reasoning makes creative companionship with parents ever more desirable.

get into father and mother are the ones they can turn to for understanding and help, and that though their behavior may be disapproved as unwise or unsuitable, their parents will not stop loving them because of it.

Among the studies that give us hints about how to be of help to our children are some that show how valuable are opportunities for using initiative. Having such opportunities means first of all, the absence of rigid, repressive discipline. To be able to do things on his own, without being criticized for lack of ex-pertness, gives a child a sense of personal dignity. Tom is likely to do a better job of cleaning the basement if his father says, "Make your own plan of how you're going to rearrange these shelves after you've washed them," than if he stands over him and directs every move. Of *course* Tom's father thinks his plan would be better! But he knows Tom thinks *his* plan is best, too, and he wants Tom to get the job done and enjoy doing it. He'll be readier to take on the next job!

We want children who are lively and original, not just carbon copies of the "average" child! What we have is at least partly up to us—to our way of handling our children. If we put them on their own a lot and allow them to use their initiative, we're likely to see the results in their original ideas.

Your face will probably be red sometimes, when your children's ingenuity takes the form of freer activities than your neighbors allow their boys and girls; when their investigations lead the neighbor's children to come home with wet feet (from boating experiments) or torn clothes (from tree climbing), acquired while very willingly following the leader.

But take heart. Though you may be looked upon dubiously for a time by people who want children to conform, to do everything exactly as they are told, your courage will be rewarded. Your children will develop judgment, along with height and weight. Always presuming, of course, that they have been taught such basic things as property rights.

If stability is one of our goals, then opportunities for experiences that encourage some freedom of action must be part of our parental plan. The values of different experiences are hard to measure when we are close up to them, especially if they are annoying or embarrassing to adults. The mother who is very dependent on what other people do or think wants her children to wear the "right" clothes, do the "proper" things. But if overalls are what Jerry wants to wear, who are we to deny the possible values of his decision?

The opposite of giving children chances to use initiative, that is, being too watchful and solicitous, may keep children so immature that their school adjustment is affected. It will pay, though, to keep in mind what have been called children's natural powers of recovery from adults' well-meant misdirection.

Each child will be "himself," no matter what we do. Our part is to observe early and try to understand what special innate tendencies each one has. When we *know* Johnny we can tell better how to help him develop some of his natural inclinations, and soften others that seem less useful.

HOW DISCIPLINE AND PUNISHMENT DIFFER

Sometimes, of course, a child's decisions, while not made in deliberate disobedience, are so hasty and based on so little experience that trouble results. Often that trouble is enough to make the child think twice before doing a similar thing. Isn't this one of the purposes of punishment? But in this case we are relieved of having to inflict it ourselves!

However, consequences can't always be relied on to bring the regret that will prevent an act's being repeated, or to make a child more thoughtful. An 8-year old who eats more candy than we have said he should have won't always have a stomach ache. For the 10-year-old who "forgets" to come home after school to change to old clothes there are no sure-fire consequences. If Ann tears her good dress, and has to wear it patched for months, she may learn to be more careful to follow family rules. But we can't count on that sort of thing happening, so sensible parents try to build a *desire* in their children to behave in ways that work out well for them and everyone else.

Children need to have some rules to guide them. Not dozens, which restrict their activities in all directions, but a few clear ones, such as the times when they are expected to show up at home, the boundaries within which they should play, the home duties that are theirs. It is more comfortable to know what one can and can't do than to be uncertain.

CHILDREN MUST UNDERSTAND OUR AIMS

If our plan is to work, our children must understand the rules. If we punish hastily and thoughtlessly we may only make a child sulky, instead of sorry. Scolding Ann for having stayed too long when she went to play with Mary, without even giving her a chance to say whether she tried to phone home, may make her resentful. Denying her the privilege of going next time, if she's late after having been warned, is more logical; it may make her try to be more cooperative in the future.

THE CHILD BETWEEN 11 AND 12

Physical growth and skills. Last wrist bone appears in boys. Girls falling behind boys somewhat in physical strength and endurance; can no longer compete with them on equal terms. Menstruation occurs in a few girls. May be strongly individual in liking for different games and play involving motor skills.

Social progress. Membership in clubs and groups increasing in importance. Enjoy taking part in school, neighborhood, and community affairs, like "drives." Team games are very popular. Shyness, if present, may be becoming more noticeable.

Intellectual growth and activities. Begins to be critical of own artistic products. Can understand human reproduction. Understands need of care in using towels, glasses, public toilets; also importance of using handkerchief to cover coughs and sneezes. May for some time have been interested in earning money. Small earnings will allow him some independence in spending for hobbies.

Denial of privileges can be done in such a way that a child sees he is being treated according to the immature way he has acted. He can be helped to understand why he has to forfeit the right to decide for himself this time. We can also do it harshly, leaving a child thinking we are mean and vindictive.

We often punish without knowing it. Our displeasure is so plain that words are unnecessary; a look is enough to let a child know that this is something about which his mother or father feels keenly. Psychological punishment, in which we show our disappointment or disapproval, is pretty generally practiced. It can be helpful, or it can be terribly damaging, depending OD the way it is done. To show our disapproval of a child's disregard of the rights of others is not only legitimate but necessary. To cloud his happiness all day by overblaming him and harking back to the incident is another matter. To be denied his parents' esteem is strong medicine and should be used accordingly, in tiny doses. Not too close together, either. When disapproval is shown, a child needs to be taken back very promptly into the warmth of his parents' regard.

It is often remarked that we should make it clear to a child that we disapprove of his *misdeed,* not of *him.* We can say, and mean it, "You are a fine person. This thing you did was not worthy of you. Be yourself and you'll be O. K." We can show that we think he'll do better next time. The point is to strengthen his belief in himself.

Believing in a child, and constantly loving him, will do away with the need for much punishment. If a child hasn't his parents' backing he has to hunt up some kind of safe retreat from the hurt of disbelief. Study of children indicates that much punishment may tend to make them turn away from reality to a world of dreams, where they can find comfort in pretending these cruel parents aren't really their own.

If withdrawal of approval serves as a punishment, so does giving of approval become a reward. People sometimes talk disapprovingly of rewards for good behavior, meaning, of course, material rewards like presents or money. Children who are really in harmony with their parents don't need such rewards, and it is too bad to introduce them.

It's quite a different matter to say, "You've been such a help at home all week that there's extra time. Let's go to the movies together," or, "You picked out the vegetables you bought so carefully you can have what you saved to put in your bank." Unexpected, unplanned rewards in the form of pleasant surprises help to keep a child's morale high.

There is one form of reward none of us can get along without —sincere appreciation. We mothers get it in the form of cries of delight when we bake a chocolate cake, or the look in the eye of a husband who finds his pet tie freshly pressed. Rewards are what we make them. A parent who doesn't dare step in the door after being down town without an offering of candy or a toy has made something bad of them.

Promises to reward are a risky business. "A dollar, if your report card is better next month" may bring results, but not always the kind we want. It may bring cheating; it may bring dismay to a child already doing his level best; it may even bring a slump in the marks because the child gets tense and frightened trying for the reward that for him has to take the place of real encouragement.

Physicians judge that about one-third of all the people who consult them have nothing actually wrong with their bodies as far as the physicians can tell. There is no doubt, though, that these people suffer. They have all kinds of things the matter with them, but they are not definite *physical* ailments. Rather, their trouble is in their emotional life.

How did they get that way? Somehow, somewhere along the road of their experience they have picked up a load of fear and worry and anxiety that has finally grown so big as to be unbearably heavy. The person is ill in spirit no matter how husky his frame. Sometimes these anxieties are associated with things that happened away back in childhood, with situations that could have been straightened out if the parents had only known what was bothering the child. If we more often passed over little things in a child's behavior we wouldn't run the risk of having him worry unnecessarily about whether he is respected and accepted.

Sometimes, of course, what children worry about are things their parents have had no hand in. Such happenings can be counterbalanced by the gaiety, humor, and atmosphere of happiness that prevails at home.

An example of the way in which a parent can unconsciously contribute to a child's tendency to be overly concerned about himself may occasionally be seen in reactions toward illness. Mrs. A, for example, may lay great stress on illness. She is constantly worrying over the slightest symptom, popping her child into bed, and calling the doctor needlessly. It would come as a great shock to her to hear that she may be doing this because she resents her child and doesn't actually like the responsibility involved in his care; that what on the surface looks like love and deep interest may really be an effort to suppress her annoyance at having to care for a child. Is she not "grownup" enough to want responsibility? As a girl, did she have too much of the care of her younger brothers and sisters?

That, if true, is sad enough. But see what it may do to her child. It may make *him* all through life use illness as a way of getting attention. Sensing but not understanding his mother's

THE CHILD BETWEEN 12 AND 13

Physical growth and skills. Games involving whole body activity, like run-sheep-run, on the decline. Capable of carrying out good personal hygiene habits. Muscles have grown to represent 40 to 45 percent of body weight. Parts of the hip bone unite in girls. Has 24 or 26 permanent teeth. May show self-consciousness about trying to learn new feats of physical skill. If too unlike mates in size or maturity, boy or girl may be conscious of awkwardness; girls may be quite conscious of their maturing figures. Choice of activities more and more influenced by individual preferences. Many, from now on, tend to be spectators at many games and sports.

Social progress. Social contacts constantly widening; independence in choice of friends more noticeable. If conditions surrounding child are unfavorable, beginnings of juvenile delinquency may occur. Lack of experience and practice in motor skills may have resulted in child's becoming an onlooker instead of an active participant in games. As puberty approaches, child may crave periods of being alone. Boys admire other boys who are skillful, bold, and daring. Girls, to be looked up to, must "conform," be feminine and ladylike.

Intellectual growth and activities. Can add and subtract decimals. Ability to reason is markedly on the increase. Understands abstract ideas like "justice" "honesty" etc. Can postpone satisfactions; emotional outbursts when his desires are thwarted and becoming infrequent. Similarity of interests and mental age increasingly influence the choice of friends. Interest constantly growing in the culture in which they live—the contributions of the past, how science affects it, etc. Awareness of moral codes (shown by interest in living up to those embodied in Camp Fire or Scout work). Religious interests prominent in many children, but religious ideas usually still accepted uncritically. As adolescence approaches, sympathetic understanding by parents is of prime importance to successful adjustment.

feelings, he uses a device, sickness, to get her to make a great fuss over him.

Another example of how a parent's perfection-seeking attitudes sometimes hamper a child is in connection with social pressures that we take too seriously. We overimpress upon children how necessary it is to be clean and presentable, how some things are or are not "done" ("don't belch"; "say 'thank you' "), losing sight of the child's immaturity, and need to pick up these bits of learning gradually.

WHEN THE EMPHASIS IS MISPLACED

It is very easy, in our zeal for giving good training, to attach too much importance to some things, or to the wrong ones. Just as our frowning on belching would seem queer to those Orientals for whom this is socially acceptable, so it would seem absurd to us, if we stopped to think, to encourage a child to think of his genital organs with disgust. And yet that is what many a mother risks doing when she expresses disgust over a little child's dabbling in his urine or bowel movements.

What has this to do with a 6-year-old or a 12-year-old? Just this. The "forgotten" happenings of childhood have been stored up, not in his memory, where they may easily be brought to light, but deeper, in his feelings. If he has been made to feel guilty over this, or any other idea that his parents imparted forcibly, he may feel unnatural and unnecessary restraint throughout his life. In many women who are frigid, to whom sexual intercourse is distasteful, this feeling may have had its start in the emphasis placed upon the disagreeable nature of the body's waste products. Because of the location of the genital organs, the feeling has come to be associated with them.

A child may become oversensitive to dirt and germs. He takes so seriously chance remarks about them that he can scarcely enjoy a meal away from home. He must in adult life scrub the restaurant silver before eating, and search his plate or glass for thumb marks. Another child, hearing that milk is a frequent carrier of infection, becomes so disgusted that he declares, and believes always, that he "doesn't like" milk.

We call people who have such aversions "fussy," a term that doesn't go below the surface. Really, their fear or distaste is deep-seated and unhealthy.

A child whose parents make too many demands is likely himself to become conscious of and ready to criticize the mistakes and shortcomings of others. Overanxiety about whether one is living up to the expectations of parents may result in odd behavior that seems to have little or no relation to the underlying trouble. If we want our children to accept and enjoy other people we ourselves should accept them as children. To try to make our children over into something they are not, to urge on them an ideal pattern of behavior that we have somehow set up in our minds, is unfair. Fortunately, most parents like their children too much to try any such tactics.

INFLUENCES OF HAPPY HOME SURROUNDINGS

There would be little point in trying to describe an ideal home, because such widely different kinds of environment produce splendid results. One thing we are pretty sure of, though, is that what children need for happiness (aside from the kind of parents they have) is a place where children can be *children.*

This at once rules out a house that caters only to grownups. If great importance is attached to polished furniture, then the child must be limited so much in his actions that he misses much of the fun of being a child. The exchange of the old-fashioned chilly parlor for the living room of today is a symbol of our altered feeling about family needs.

Actually, the *atmosphere* of a home matters quite as much as the size. There are happy families living in trailers, and there are keenly unhappy ones with more rooms than they know what to do with.

Our society has paid little attention to the need for privacy for individual family members. Houses and apartments have grown steadily smaller. They're easier to care for, but people have to rub up against each other too much. A good deal of ingenuity has to be used to see that children, as they grow older, can retire from the family group when they want to. When space is very limited it becomes extra important for each child to have some place of his own, even though it's only a desk in a corner, or some shelves or drawers beside his bed. If there is no basement work room, the kitchen will often have to be set aside for such use. It takes a lot of patience and self-control to live squeezed up together like seeds in a pod.

Housing is one of our really desperate problems. It is ironical even to say that each child needs a room of his own when millions of families are living in wretched conditions of overcrowding, are barely existing in shacks and trailers, and in miserable old houses that should long since have been pulled down. How can we expect to raise mentally healthy children when whole families have to live in a single room, sharing toilet facilities with perhaps 20 other families?

However, there are brighter sides to the picture. More and more families, when they build, buy, or rent a home of their own, move to the edge of town, or outside, because they recognize children's needs of space and air and freedom. Housing developments are providing playgrounds. The family car has made possible a great increase in family enjoyment through jaunts and trips. Such shared pleasures may help to take the place in children's memories of a family home, lived in for many years.

Parents can do a lot toward inspiring traditions that will endure, like family celebrations of holidays, birthdays, and other special occasions. These may help to substitute for the security built up by long-continued life in one community.

Because of the earlier exposure of children today to outside influences like radio and pictures that come into their homes from the very earliest years, some ways must be found of emphasizing the values that can come only through family life. The emotional satisfactions of home must be great if they are to compete with the forces that are pulling families apart

Only the family can give children what they need as a start toward becoming fine human beings. The responses a child learns in his family set the tone of his feelings toward people. Even when he is reproved or punished it will not be in the coldly impersonal way of the outside world. He senses that it is because his parents *care* about him, that it is because his welfare means so much to them that they correct his mistakes and wrong-doing. If he is wanted and cherished here he can face life with greater confidence, even when his skin color or his name is "different."

When you see the eagerness with which children set out for a Sunday hike with their father you wish it could happen oftener. When he plays games with them, whether baseball or rummy, a man has a chance to learn what his children are like. Working with them shows him one side of them, playing with them another. The more, and the earlier, a father enters into the life of his boys and girls, the better he is able to understand them, and contribute to their growth. What he gives them by his companionship is specially welcomed because feminine influences so largely prevail in American homes and schools. What they give *him* is beyond measure, as fathers will agree. A man who is bringing up a family of children is constantly being surprised at the way they are influencing his personality.

HOW CAN WE PROVIDE STABILITY?

Some of us can remember a time when family life was more stable than it *is* today. To the millions of children and young people who have no chance to put down roots in any one place we owe a great debt. Somehow we must create for them something to take the place of more permanent and secure ways of life.

Nowadays, even in a neighborhood in which many families own their own homes, only 1 child out of 15 or 20 may have lived in the same house ever since he was born. In a great city, many families move every year, or even oftener. With increasing numbers of tenant farmers, farm families, too, are on the move. Under these conditions family treasures and heirlooms—what H. L. Mencken calls "the sacred rubbish" of the family— are largely lacking. How can we give children a sense of "belonging," a sense of the enduring nature of family life? If there are few familiar, cherished possessions, symbols of his family's life in the past, does a child miss some stimulus that comes to him through pride in his ancestors? American families have come here from all over the world. But to become Americans does not mean that we should let our family traditions fade out of mind any more than we would let the precious strip of embroidery made by a great-grandmother fade.

Perhaps the fact that there are more grandfathers and grandmothers alive today is one thing that helps children feel the ongoing nature of family life. Grandparents should be encouraged in story-telling about their youth, and in recreating the past for children through old songs.

Parents who have to move from place to place can make a wholehearted effort to be warmly friendly to their children's new acquaintances. Boys and girls whose ties are frequently broken need to have a home that invites the making of new ones.

But new ties can't be formed unless new neighbors are generous and friendly. Those who are secure and established in a community may thoughtlessly fail to accept newcomers. Especially when migration means a mixing of people who have very different backgrounds and customs, the more settled community members may turn up their noses at ways with which they are unfamiliar. Their children can easily develop feelings of being "better" than their neighbors. The children of both groups are hurt by such unfriendliness, but the bruises show more on those who are inspected critically, on the children who are made to feel that they don't fit in.

Who can ease such hurts or prevent them? Those families that have been less buffeted about have an obligation to do something constructive in their neighborhoods. Such parents can do a lot to back up the efforts of schools, which are finding many ways of encouraging real brotherhood. All groups have much with which to enrich the lives of other groups. By sharing with each other our music, art, dancing, special foods, and other traditional folkways we add to our enjoyment and understanding.

Most of our schools are trying their level best to dig out the ugly prejudices that are the result of narrowness and ignorance. We parents need to find out more about how we can help. For one thing, we can guard our words. Expressions that belittle others, used because we hear them so commonly rather than because we believe them, should be kept strictly out of our speech. Love of our neighbors should be shown in our everyday living, in our acts—such as the way we vote—as well as in our words. Because harmful fears and suspicions of peoples, races, religions, and political ideas are harder to get rid of than poison ivy, we need to give our help to all the agencies that are working out methods of fighting evil forces. Each individual family that does all in its power, even though the visible results seem small, is having a hand in the education that may help to save us from disaster.

Many of us suffer from a false notion about "the good old days." In the first place, they were not good—for enough people. In the second place, they are not going to return. Let's not try to escape our obligation to our children:

> We must bring up our children so that they expect and like to work out their own problems, instead of yielding to others who may try to force them into accepting ready-made solutions. We must at the same time help them to see the need of being able to work with others toward common ends, and not to be too stiffnecked to accept new ideas and ways of living.

Most of us parents can hear echoes out of our childhood urging us to "be good." We even make those echoes ring over again, without thinking, when we say to our children, "Be a good boy!" or, "Have you been a good girl?"

If we stopped to ask ourselves what we mean by such cautions, we'd have to admit they are tinged with a dread of *bad* behavior! They are really a sort of warning to a child not to do anything we might be ashamed of or blamed for! Parents are only human; they dislike to have anything happen that will reflect on them. When their Louis or Paul breaks a neighbor's window or scratches his car fender, they feel that it's not to their credit as parents, so it hurts their pride.

It's not strange that we look on our children as extensions of ourselves, and want their doings to make us show up well. But it *is* strange that we are so blind about it, always fooling ourselves into thinking that what we do is for our children's good, when really, deep down, it's as much, or more, for our satisfaction or our reputation.

"GOODNESS" IS A BYPRODUCT

Actually, children turn out better if less weight is placed upon "goodness" than on seeing to it that conditions under which they live are such that "goodness," happiness, and all-around fine adjustment will be the natural results. Strain and tension come in when our attitudes show distrust of a child's good intent.

If we're too eager for our children to be "good" we easily fall into habits of being critical. Because obedience used to be so much stressed, we unconsciously follow along, forgetting that what we *really* want is for children to develop standards of their own that will stay with them, rather than to be little puppets that are jerked on a string in tune with someone else's ideas. Children who are brought up to respond like clockwork to rules we have laid down have little chance to gain the strength that comes from self-handling of problems.

If Hilda follows her parents' dictates too passively, she may place too much reliance on the judgment of her new friends when she goes away from home for the first time. Marie, whose parents gave her more chances to think for herself, profited by some of the mistakes she made (like the time she had to wear for several years a coat she'd insisted on getting, but soon tired of).By the time she's on her own she's developed pretty good judgment, and doesn't have to ask her friends' advice about every little thing.

WHY ENCOURAGE INDEPENDENCE?

Besides the absence of training in self-reliance that goes with too much pressure on "obedience" there is the possibility that a strong-willed, bright child may be tempted into an outer show of submission while inwardly he rebels. This is almost bound to cause unhappiness later. For when such a child reaches an age when stirrings toward independence are very urgent he may suddenly break down the fence of his parents' restraint. His father and mother are puzzled and hurt. He has kept his feelings to himself; they have had no notion of the inner conflict under his hitherto submissive behavior.

Ted, whose parents have had "no trouble at all" with him, suddenly at the age of 12 takes to going with boys his folks disapprove of; or he doesn't turn up after school until long after the usual time, and refuses to give any explanation of where he has been. He has come to the conclusion his parents can no longer "make" him do the things he has been submitting to; the boys his family thinks are "a good influence" may want to play football while he prefers to build radio sets. He may have found a boy they don't know whose lively mind and interests match his own.

What seems like sudden rebellion is really the breaking out of a fire that has been smoldering a long time.

It can happen that parents, with the best of intentions, make a child become deceitful in efforts to escape domination.

Eleven-year old Edna, more mature than most girls of her age, tells her mother she is going to Ruth's house to study, when really she is at the drug store with Elinor, an older girl who has a glamorous attraction for her because she knows how to joke and fool with the boys. It's no use for Edna to ask if she may do this; she knows well enough her mother would be shocked at the mere idea of her being interested in boys. In another case, Chuck, whose father has told him he was too young to have a gun, saves up money for one which he keeps at John's house.

This is not to say that Edna's parents should let her run wild, or that Chuck's should weakly give in to his every request. Rather, they need to be aware of the changes that are bound to come with development, and of how absurd it is to expect to rule all their children's doings. Both sets of parents, and the rest of us, need to remember that some sort of "protest" behavior is necessary during the growing-up period. Even youngsters who are thoroughly happy in their home life, who need not struggle for independence, "feel their oats" on occasion, and kick up their heels accordingly.

HOW CHARACTER DEVELOPS

We all want our children to grow up law abiding and honest, with high moral standards and character. But to believe that there is any special training magic that will produce "character" is to be disappointed. We can't bring up a child of whom we will be proud by following any set of hard-and-fast rules.

What we *can* do is to make it more satisfying to our children to do right than wrong; we can give them plenty of enjoyable practice in doing acceptable things. We can try to keep from shaping their attitudes by pressures coming from our own sometimes very set ways of thinking or acting, like social or political prejudices. We can be so fair in our treatment of them that they will not be pushed into doing wrong through fear.

Take cheating in school, for example. Why do children cheat? For a great variety of reasons. Because they think their teacher is unfair; because they want to make as good a showing as some other child; because they are afraid of punishment for failure, among others. A child may cheat in spelling, because spelling is hard for him, and yet have no inclination at all to cheat in arithmetic, because that comes easy to him. One may cheat in a game who would not think of doing so when money was involved. Honesty, or dishonesty, appears in specific situations. It is not a large, general way of behaving applying to everything a child does.

A child's home is the first influence on his moral development, and the one that never lets up. There he is exposed to four different kinds of help: the example of his parents; their preaching and urging; reproof and punishment when he does wrong; and the pleasant and stimulating effects of actions that result in his getting warm approval. There, in the home, the underlying capacities of the child need a chance to develop. We must be as careful not to get in the way of character development as we are about directing it.

HOW CHILDREN LEARN MORAL LAWS

Learning to be honest and upright follows the same pattern as other kinds of learning: it takes place when children find satisfaction in doing right (whether the happiness their parents show, or their own joy at having lived up to what was expected of them); when they find that poor behavior brings sorrow or pain (but this can be carried too far, as when a child lies because he has suffered severe punishment and fears it will be repeated); or when the consequences of desirable behavior are pleasant.

When parents are careless and lax and have no consistent plan of guidance, conditions are right for children to "get by" with things they know are wrong. The importance of our own personal moral habits and attitudes can't be overlooked. Because we get at the child first, and he unconsciously accepts our ways as "the" ways, we parents have an enormous advantage over any future influences.

Also a very grave responsibility. We have to be careful that the things we stress are the really important ones. A boy may grow into manhood with perfect table manners, but with very little sense of keeping his obligations to the very same people he is polite to. If his mother has emphasized the one and neglected the other, can he be blamed for acting as if it were more important to jump from his chair every time his mother comes into a room than to keep his word to her?

By the time children are passing through the elementary grades they are being deluged, of course, with all manner of other influences. Other children are probably next most important to parents in helping to form a child's character. Because they want to be liked and admired, children follow the leader a good deal; the influence of friends on conduct is very marked in the schoolroom and in group play. But what one does when influenced by the spirit of the group may not match up with his behavior when away from the crowd. Jim may join his neighborhood gang in throwing stones at street lights when he would never think of doing such a thing by himself.

That the effect of such follow-the-leader behavior is often short-lived may be a comfort to parents who must, temporarily perhaps, have to live in a neighborhood where the children's morale is not high. It has been found that as the group changes, standards change, too; so temporary contacts need not necessarily be a cause of great alarm providing a child's home background is good. Natalie is not going to turn into a pickpocket because the little girls she plays with in the second grade give her the idea of taking home colored chalk from school. Jack's parents may be taken by surprise when he is reported as one of a group that has been scrawling filthy words on the school lavatory walls, but it doesn't mean that he's going to be a sex pervert.

If some of Jack's and some of Natalie's companions keep on doing wrong things it will be largely because of the way their acts are looked on at home. Her mistake is an isolated one for Natalie, because her ideas about honesty are clearer after her parents' discussion of how careful we must be not to take things that do not belong to us. Another child's mother may smooth over the dishonesty, saying, "The school has lots of chalk, anyway we're taxpayers." Jack's escapade may be used well, or poorly, as a ground for home teaching. His father can explain to him how natural boys' curiosity about sex is and how smutty words or stories, used in the hope of impressing others, are often a confession of ignorance, thus making the whole thing seem silly and "young" rather than "bad." Or, he can punish his son harshly, leaving him with the feeling that sex is dirty and disgraceful.

We come back over and over to the home as the most important influence in a child's life. The home interprets what a child picks up outside, solidly backing up his outside learning when it is good. When family standards and ideals are high, the child is more likely to question ways that don't measure up to them.

IT'S THE MORAL "CLIMATE" THAT MATTERS

Parents who demand special favors, who use roundabout methods of getting what they want, such as accepting "rakeoffs" or seeking out the "right people" who can save them money by outwitting the law, are doing their children great harm. The children may, because of this experience, sink into the habit of excusing themselves for sharp or crooked practices, with the idea that *their* needs are special, that favors are their natural right.

Attitudes, once absorbed, are as hard to remove as it is to get ink out of a blotter. Because we parents are largely unaware of our prejudices and special slants of thinking, we pass them on in ignorance of what we are doing. When they disagree with what a child is learning outside, he becomes confused; like the child who said, "When I'm at school, I believe the way my teacher says we should. But when I go home, what my parents say seems right."

We have to be especially careful about our very human tendency to build ourselves up at the expense of others, which, if we are insecure, we are sometimes betrayed into doing. If any group in a community is very much in the minority, those who belong to the larger groups sometimes belittle the few as "different." Whether the group be newcomers to America, people of an unfamiliar religious faith, are "capitalists" or "labor groups" or belong to another race, the damage to our children of accepting hasty, ignorant opinions about them is the same.

"Helping children to enter imaginatively into the lives and feelings of others is at the basis of all good character-education in both home and school," says S. R. Laycock. "To come to treat all other human beings as one's brothers involves the keen realization that other human beings have the same needs and the same capacity for feelings as oneself."

If we can bring about in our children such feelings of well-being and such a sense of perspective and fairness that they are not always having to measure themselves against others, we shall have gone a long way toward strengthening their moral fibre. What we want is for them to hate injustice and wrong, and to love truth and honor. We cannot expect to keep illogical emotional reactions entirely out of their lives, but we can help them at least to be flexible in their thinking.

Our children will have courage to lift up their voices for causes that are good and just—but that may be unpopular—only if we imprint on their minds clear images of what "good" is. Such images will largely be reflections of our own behavior.

4

How families influence their children's social adjustment

When a child's relation with his parents is warm and happy, he has a good chance of making easy, pleasant contacts outside his home. But families may be very happy in their relationships within the home and still not provide the kind of atmosphere that helps their children to make good adjustment outside.

What might be called the in-growing family is an instance of this. Parents can become too absorbed in their children to see that family life should be a part of something larger. We can enjoy our children and each other so much that we cut ourselves off from valuable experiences outside the family. Sooner or later will come regrets. The children will grow restless. They won't want to continue this close-knit companionship forever. Home may begin to seem like a cage even though now it is hard for them to know how to get along outside the cage. Jane loves, while she is little, to go on trips with her parents, to be included in every plan they make. But as she approaches adolescence, when she begins to need close friends and crave social life that includes boys, she may be at a loss to know how to squeeze her way into the school circle that seems to be having such fun.

There is another kind of family, happy in its own relationships, but timid about social contacts.

Mona, though very bright, finds it an ordeal to speak in class. Hers is more than the natural shyness so common among children, and so endearing. She is so bashful that she has few friends. Other girls mistake her shyness for standoffishness, and so don't go out of their way to be friendly. Her failure to enter into things is in all likelihood copied from her parents; they don't entertain much, rarely mix in crowds, and have strongly individual interests with which they are content.

We may be tempted to say that Mona inherited her shyness. It is just as probable that it is only her lack of exposure to social life which has kept Tier from learning ways of easy companionship and adaptability. Environment has been as much, if not more, responsible than heredity.

THE FAMILY IN A LARGER FAMILY-THE COMMUNITY

We must look to our own ways if we are interested in seeing our children fit comfortably into the world in which they are going to live. If we simply assume that they will find their place as a matter of course, both they and we may be disappointed.

The part we take in community life will have a good deal to do with the way our children are accepted. Children who are "leaders" at school, who are looked up to, are more likely than not to come from homes where their interests are encouraged, and where family members have interesting lives.

Parents can make the mistake of being too anxious for their children to show up well. A child is unfortunate whose mother sends him or her to school conspicuously well dressed, or who gives such elaborate parties that other children are afraid to invite her little girl to their simple ones. A parent—usually a mother—who makes too earnest efforts to increase her child's popularity may end by having her child disliked.

To see one's child really left out hurts. Studying such a child's personality may be rewarding. If Jack is unpopular because he's a poor sport, his parents need to ask themselves if he got this way because they made things too easy for him. Is Winnie bumptious because, unthinkingly, her parents have given her a false idea of her ability or importance? Perhaps they have praised her when her efforts didn't warrant praise.

WHEN WE KEEP THE DOORS OPEN

There's one way in which parents can weight the scale in favor of a child's good social adjustment—by making their home a friendly place. They can make it a center where there are opportunities to do interesting things; where the kitchen is not too tidy for corn-popping; where the grownups laugh with the children, or turn the lights low and tell ghost stories with lots of places for shrieks in them.

Being treated with respect keeps children's morale high. Interest in each other's activities is one way of encouraging social growth. This implies sharing discussions of things that matter; a father who never talks about his business affairs at home can hardly expect his children to talk about *their* affairs.

We can take a more intelligent interest in children's doings if we know something of what is going on in their inner lives. Then, instead of being annoyed by Mary's absorption in movie stars, we will recognize her need of models to copy, and perhaps be able to help her to find worthy ones—in books, girls' organizations, and friends.

Knowing what children are like at different ages will help us to be more understanding about the differences in social maturity of boys and girls. We won't be so impatient over Fred's greater interest in his baseball nine than in the dancing class his older sister found delightful at the same age.

One feature of family life which is related to good social adjustment has been the subject of little thought. This is the age of the parents. Particularly among those parents who married late, or whose children came late, some attention should be paid to seeing that the children have a normal social life. Not all older people are set in their ways and averse to change. But it sometimes happens that parents, fast reaching the point where they enjoy peace and quiet, tend to frown on boisterousness, noise, and what seems to them the "silly" behavior of childhood.

Without meaning to they may discourage their children from bringing their friends home. They are more apt than younger parents to be overanxious about their children's safety. By their hovering, protective attitude they may deny their youngsters experiences they need. Amy's parents hang back from letting her be one of a foursome of girls and boys who want to go to a movie together, not realizing that at 11 she is as mature in many ways as her mother was at 14.

TO BE ACCEPTED, CHILDREN
NEED TO "ACT THEIR AGE"

Few things interfere with a child's acceptance by his peers like immaturity. One who is immature emotionally, who cries or is angered easily, may get a cold shoulder. Nothing is worse, in a boy's mind, than to be called a "sissy." A child's urge to grow up is sometimes at war with his parents' urge to keep him under their thumb. His efforts to establish himself may be in part rebellion at this.

What an inescapable stage that of fist fights seems to be. And how parents deplore it! But fighting is a way of proving that you are no longer a baby, no longer dependent on "mama." Strength and toughness are traditional possessions of boys and men. Tommy has probably been told dozens of times that "boys don't cry, they are brave."

How better can he show his toughness than by having fights? He has to impress himself on other boys in *some* way. The ones who can run fastest, climb highest, throw a ball the farthest are likely to be the most admired. The one who shows he can "take it" in a fight is respected by his companions.

Then there is the fact that some bigger boys "pick on" small ones in order to show they are smarter and tougher, and in general prove their superiority. The small ones pick on each other. The more secure and sure of himself a child feels, the less his need of asserting himself in this way; but most boys, even those who have little or no impulse to boast of physical supremacy, will be called upon sooner or later to hold their own, and show that they are unafraid physically.

A child who has been forbidden by his parents to fight is in a dilemma. If he obeys his parents he will be considered a coward; if he disregards them he will be scolded at home.

If we can remember that this primitive way of settling disputes is a phase that passes quickly, and that it takes stout courage to stand up to physical pain, we shall be less likely to set conflict in our child's mind by showing that we are disturbed by fighting.

Only occasionally does it seem wise for parents to step in. If they constantly put their oar in they may make their child suffer much more than he would from any physical hurt. It will not be to his advantage to learn to lean on someone else's help in settling matters; he should take care of himself. Even in handling the case of the typical "bully" who habitually lords it over children younger or weaker than himself, it is as necessary to find the reasons for the offending child's behavior as it is to protect the others. To stop him puts only a temporary end to the trouble. To probe into the reasons why he wants this kind of relationship is more constructive; for by uncovering the roots of the bully's problem it may be possible to do away with the *cause* of his behavior.

The child who is popular in school is one who is somewhat aggressive, in the socially approved sense of the word. This implies parents who aren't so dominating that they have flattened all the life out of their child. Those who are popular in a group have been found to be the ones who are enthusiastic and lively. They stand out because they have strong personalities.

But in child-to-child relations other things count, as well. Children in the middle grades who are good looking, who look neat, who are happy, friendly, and smiling are apt to be well liked. The latter qualities probably make more difference than looks.

Peter, for example, may be a very lovable and interesting child, but if he is so quiet that no one in his school room knows what an expert swimmer he is, he's not likely to be much admired. If May is so conscious of the braces on her teeth that she tries to keep from smiling or laughing, the other children won't have a chance to learn how friendly she really is.

Children who play fair, who are "good sports," are welcomed and liked by other children. Parents have a lot to do with developing this kind of behavior. If we take a child's part on every occasion we deny him the chance to learn to take small defeats and unfairness as a part of life. Sooner or later he is going to run up against situations beyond his control where he will have to accept unfair treatment. He should be able to do so without sulking or self-pity.

Parents can build up a child's belief in himself. Each time he becomes good at something his ability to succeed at other things is strengthened.

Viola, who has had no chance to learn to swim, may hesitate about trying in a group of children who are old hands at it. But if she is good, say, on roller skates, or has some other physical skill, her general self-confidence will help her over the hump.

By the time children are 12 a change has taken place in what children look for in each other, studies tell us. A boy can now look as unkempt as he pleases and still be rated "tops" as a companion if he's good at group games and is a "regular boy." But it is more important for girls, by this time, to "conform." If they are ladylike and demure, careful about their appearance and intent on following the Emily Post pattern they are much more sure of being liked by other girls, provided they are also friendly. (How much are these notions as to what is important influenced by stress placed on them at home?)

"BELONGING" IS ALL-IMPORTANT

When a child goes to school, he feels lost indeed among a group that contains so many older children, unless he can become a part of his own age group. He needs to be accepted by his roommates, must have a feeling of "belonging" if he is to be comfortable and happy. He needs to share their interests, to have children to laugh with, to show off to, to gain ascendancy over, and to knuckle down to.

It will take a little longer for a child who is shy, or timid about physical feats, to feel he's a part of the group than for one who is active and self-confident. There will be leaders, who are strongly out-going in their nature, and there will be children whose role it is to attach themselves to the leaders. One child may start 90 percent of the activities of the group. His ideas are so good, and his manner so tactful that the others accept his taking the initiative in good spirit. Others, not so original, may be liked for their ready cooperation.

Dot, the 10-year-old, listens conscientiously to a certain radio program because she wants to be acceptable to Lora and Sue, who have talked about it. Six-year-old Harry tries to write on the blackboard with his right hand, which is unnatural and wrong for him, because he doesn't want to be "different."

When a child goes to school he begins to see that other homes have different standards, ideas, and practices from those he's used to. When his family's ways—what they eat, whether they use the back or the front door, the time the children must go to bed—are somewhat unlike those of others in the neighborhood, he begins to look at his home more closely. He may have a few doubts as to whether his parents are as all-wise as he supposed.

This is a perfectly healthy kind of doubt for a child to have. Life would be queerer than it is now, and adjustments would be harder to make, if all children grew up confident that their family's ways were the *only* ways. It would be as hard to get along with our neighbors as nations find it to understand and get along with each other.

This is a step in the "psychological weaning" process by which a child finally stands on his own feet. But it is hard for parents to see it going on. Few of us welcome it. One evidence of children's having one foot outside the home is their growing interest in forming groups among themselves.

By the age of 9 or 10, children want something more than to be accepted as a member of the herd. They begin to band together in small clubs or gangs or packs. It adds to a child's fun and safety and prestige to have a bunch to back him up. The Boy and Girl Scout movements recognize this impulse; their program makes something wholesome and constructive out of it. But the fact that there is a need for Cub Scout Packs suggests that the former age (12) of entrance into scouting was set too late—later than the appearance of the strong desire to belong to an intimate group.

The word "gang" has come to have such a sinister meaning that we hesitate to use it in speaking of the activities of children. But it does convey a sense of solidarity that such a word as "group" or "club" doesn't quite carry; also, this stage of wanting to run together in a pack is something so normal that the term "gang age" has been used to describe it.

THE GANG SPIRIT CAN BE PUT TO CONSTRUCTIVE USE

Neighborhood gangs fall into hoodlumism only when their natural desire for joint activity has nothing wholesome to feed on. The spirit back of the gang can be used to promote team play, good sportsmanship, and forgetfulness of self. It *is* up to parents to see that there are opportunities for safe and sane and legitimate activities. To go on hikes with a knapsack lunch, to scoop out a dugout in the backyard, or fence off a corner of the attic or basement that children can call their own, satisfies some craving so deep that we had better go along with it than to try to thwart it.

There should be some sort of medal for those mothers who, never having been boys themselves, still have enough imagination to allow their boys to use their own rooms pretty much as they like. Boys need a place where their friends feel free to gather, where no one will interfere with the radio parts that are so precious, even if they are strewn in what seems hit-or-miss

fashion. A father who sacrifices his chance to sleep late on a holiday in order to drive his son's gang up-river for a night's camping trip is going to have that son rise up and call him blessed.

Girls do not feel the urge toward strenuous athletic activities quite as strongly as boys. They are more likely to be interested in putting on plays, in painting, or in other things that take highly skilled hands. They like to bicycle, and hike, play baseball, and take part in swimming matches. But they are apt to be more interested in the social than in the competitive side of sports.

Of course, there are wide individual variations in the play interests of children. Some girls may go in for strenuous activity almost entirely and some boys may prefer quieter games. Individual differences in play activities are often greater than the differences between boys and girls.

FRIENDSHIPS

Even though he identifies himself with a group, a child is likely to have a "best friend" with whom he shares especially warmly the pleasures of the group, and with whom he by turns quarrels and makes up. Quarreling may signify the opposite of not liking a person; you like him very much, therefore what he does and thinks matters decidedly. Quarreling seems more common between good friends than between children who are indifferent to one another.

During the grade-school years children's interests have less to do with their choice of friends than the immediate availability of other children. Living in the same neighborhood, being in the same grade at school and about the same in age and development usually determines friendships. How short-lived such relations may be in the lower grades is shown by a study in which only about one-fourth of the children who named each other as "best friends" were still one another's first choice a month later.

As a child becomes older and has more interests that are personal and special, he is more "choosy" about his friends. Their tastes, their sense of humor, their feelings about many things must run along with his if the companionship is going to last.

Two children often play together better than three. Jealousy sometimes crops up when three play together, each wanting to be the only one who counts with another. It may take a good deal of ingenuity for Mary's mother to arrange things so that Nancy, the next door child, is not ignored when Joan comes to play with Mary.

Children show very different sides to their brothers and sisters than they do to other children. This makes intimates outside t¾e family very desirable. Neil is only a younger brother at home, bossed by two older sisters; outside, his ideas command some respect from his pals. Kay's mother has always encouraged close companionship between her and her sister, Martha, a year and a half older. But soon Martha will, as an adolescent, have interests that Kay is not ready for. Kay needs her own friends, so that she will neither be left high and dry when Martha begins to have dates, nor be tempted to grow up too fast.

GROWTH OF AFFECTION AND LOVE

Children between 6 and 12 are usually most absorbed in friends of the same sex. Presently they are going to begin expanding so that eventually they can love people of the other sex. Their relations with their parents have a good deal to do with how they take the steps that will lead them into mature love relationships in adult life.

It is often assumed that because boys have a strong "opposite sex" relationship from the very first—their love for their mother —they may be able to change over to mature love of the other sex more easily than girls. Girls, of course, are usually, like boys, more intimately associated with their mothers than with their fathers in early life.

Boys of the age we are interested in have, of course, moved on to the stage of being pals with their fathers. It is a healthy thing when the 8-, 9- or 10-year-old grows out of expecting his mother to tuck him in bed. Mothers sometimes cling to the old relationship; fathers enjoy having their sons show more and more manlike comradeliness.

Girls, as they get older, begin to have a feeling toward their fathers that is related to their changing needs. For a girl to be able to admire her father, and to enjoy his companionship is valuable. But if too great an attachment grows between them, in which a girl idealizes her father too much, and considers him just about perfect, it may stand in the way of her happiness-Some girls never marry, others can never be quite happy in marriage, because the image of the adored father always gets between them and other men.

Does it sound absurd, when talking about school children, to bring up such unhappy possibilities? Just because the results of being close to parents may not show until much later is one of the best of reasons for examining the kind of love we offer our children, and the kinds of responses we expect. It doesn't look like much of a problem, to be sure, when Jim says he'd rather stay at home than go to camp. When he doesn't fume over being asked to play his violin for his mother's guests we are apt to think how polite and good-natured he is. Taken by themselves these things don't seem to mean much. But, happening over and over, they might show that Jim is sticking too close to his mother. Will his wife always have to "mother" him?

Polly's father, calling her his little sweetheart and shelling out money whenever she coaxes him, is not setting up a very good pattern in her little-girl mind as to what to expect from men. It would be unfortunate if she were to grow up to be a "little-girl" woman, and expect always to be on the receiving end. It is pleasant for fathers to be *in* a position to make their daughters happy; but they want to be sure it is real happiness they are fostering, and not just selfishness.

More and more, then, during the 6 to 12 period, boys' and girls' affection will be going out to their friends. As one becomes a person in his own right, he needs to find others of his own kind to exchange confidences and experiences with.

Obviously, it is better for a child not to be limited to a single friendship. If one relationship shuts out all others, interests may be narrowed too much. One of the pair may lose interest or move away. The more a boy or girl has come to depend on his one friend, the more bereft he is going to feel.

Parents, when they see too close a tie forming, can often quietly bring about a change. Forbidding a child to play with another is about the best way of making the child absolutely necessary to him. Gentle and roundabout measures have to be taken when a child's emotions are involved. By encouraging new activities, offering new experiences, they may lessen the strength of an unhealthy, clinging-vine friendship.

WHAT CHILDREN GET FROM CAMP LIFE

A hundred years ago it would probably have seemed laughable to most Americans to be told that the time would come when children would have to be sent away from home to see a cow or a lamb or baby chickens. The need for camps for children came about when more and more children moved into cities —a big proportion of them to cities that got bigger and bigger. This meant that they were cut off from nature. They traded grass for concrete, trees for fire-escapes, flowers for paper blown about dusty streets.

Anyone can see that's not a good trade; so many people, by some hook or crook, manage to get their children into the country for a while during the summer. Camps may be the answer for those of us who haven't relatives on farms, or summer cottages by a lake.

All kinds of organizations run camps—private ones, the YM and YWCA, Girl and Boy Scouts, churches and settlements. Because a camp is expensive doesn't mean that it is good. Some of the best ones cost the least. The quality of experience for a child depends upon the people in charge, and their purpose.

All children need to rub shoulders with others. In the process, rough edges of superiority, greediness, snippiness, laziness, rudeness, and selfishness will get worn off. ("Psychological sandpapering" is what one educator aptly calls the process.) They need to see how kind, and sympathetic, and funny, and capable other children can be. At camp they learn to respect the skills they see in others, and to have the fun of being looked up to for their own special abilities.

Going to camp offers many children their first experience in being away from home, even for overnight. A child who has this experience when he is ready for it is less likely to be homesick in later years. It is not a kindness to children to let them get so rooted in their home environment that they feel unhappy when they are away.

SOME THINGS TO THINK OF IN CHOOSING A CAMP

1. Are buildings and sanitary arrangements planned so as to protect children from danger and disease?

2. Is a health report required before entrance? Is there a physician within easy reach, if not resident in the camp? Is there a registered nurse on the staff? Are there good arrange ments for isolation of ill children until it can be determined whether they are coming down with an infectious disease? Has the camp's record in regard to health been good in the past?

3. Where does the milk come from? Is it pasteurized? Are a variety of foods available? Are the meals planned by someone who knows how to provide a well-balanced diet? Have those in the kitchen been given physical examinations to make sure they are safe persons to handle foods?

4. Are the swimming arrangements safe? Are older persons with lifesaving training always in charge when the children go into the water? Are enough adults assigned to supervise so that each child is under observation all the time?

5. Are the camp directors well trained, responsible, and ma ture? Are they interested in children, or in making money? What are the ages and background experience of the counsel lors? What opportunities are there for them to spend their free time in wholesome ways?

6. Is there enough variety of projects and activities available so that each child can find things to do that he thoroughly en joys? Does the camp follow such a crowded routine that the children never have a free moment, or is there plenty of leeway for them to carry on individual interests? Is there planning for both large-group and small-group activities? Do children who enjoy doing things alone get some chance to?

7. Is the camp in question one in which great emphasis is placed on working for awards and prizes, or is there freedom from competition? Do the children feel that their attainments are being compared with those of others or does a more con structive attitude prevail, in which children are judged by their own efforts and perseverance?

5
What play means to a child

Maybe we need a new word for "play." Such a simple little word, that has such a light, trifling sound, somehow doesn't express the importance that people interested in childhood have come to attach to what it represents.

Play is the stuff of which a child's life is made. It uses every ounce of his energy. It encourages his imagination. It develops skills of both body and mind. It brings about understanding, warmth, and sympathy toward others.

How to compete, how to take hard knocks, how to win gracefully; when to assert oneself and when to forget self-interest are all learned through play. Perseverance, how to struggle through to a desired end, is as much a part of play as it is of work.

Play offers healing for hurts and sadness. It breaks down tension and releases pent-up urges toward self-expression. Play *is* the working partner of growth, for activity is as vital to growth as food and sleep.

The far-reaching significance of children's play has only lately been understood. Unless the deep-lying impulses satisfied by play are allowed to express themselves in childhood, adult life suffers. Some men and women are never able to take part freely in the life around them; they are stiff and lonely because they don't know how to mix with others. They can't lose themselves in spontaneous fun. Somehow or other their urges toward expression in play were denied the chance to come to the surface in childhood.

WHAT A CHILD'S PLAY TELLS US

The attitudes and feelings that children reveal in their play are full of meaning. A boy who plays unfairly may be reflecting his feeling of having been treated so. A child playing with dolls may act out undercurrents of jealousy of another child shown in no ether way; or such play may offer a mother lightning flashes of insight into her methods of discipline. The scoldings a child receives are often passed on to dolls or toy animals. Unsuspected feelings about parents sometimes come to light in this way, too.

A child's play is his occupation, just as surely as keeping a store or driving an engine is his father's. If he is able to use all ©f himself in his play, the change-over to whole-souled enjoyment of work happens without his having to cross any bridge. Tommy, the boy, intent on building with his blocks or perfecting his batting, turns into Thomas, the man, deep in blueprints for a building, or training a track-team.

REQUIREMENTS FOR PLAY

A "must" for play is space. There must be room for running games like tag and kick-the-can, hide and seek, and pom-pom-pullaway; the more children the more room they need. Up to tiie age of 9, children do not—nor should they—go more than a few blocks to a playground, but the community is rare that plans with this in mind. If we had built our cities with the idea of thwarting children's play we could not have done a more thorough job. No wonder children of school age have many accidents, when the streets are their only playgrounds.

The far greater freedom country children have for play is somewhat offset by the lack of outside companionship that so often goes with it. But there are incomparable advantages in being able to "whoop" and "holler'" and make use of what nature so lavishly provides in the way of play materials—brooks, and woods, rocks, caves, and wild creatures.

Up to school age, children are content with one or two play-mates, but from then on they play in larger groups. There must be chasers and chased when you play cowboy, Indians, cops and robbers. To be able to be a leader one must have a group to lead.

INTERESTS CHANGE WITH GROWTH

Mostly, the activities of the first school years are activities of the whole body; but as control of arm and leg and back muscles is gained, play that makes use of finer coordination becomes more common—marbles, jacks, handicraft of all sorts. With growth of the mind comes interest in games that involve quick-wittedness and memory—card games, word games, and checkers. Parents who play such games with their children are doing more than add to family jollity and harmony; they are broadening their children's vocabularies, helping them get a "head start" in arithmetic, and giving them practice in the art of good sportsmanship.

Children become more and more interested in turning out finished products. The model airplane, the home-made boat that really "works," the doll clothes, all put together clumsily at first, become gradually more skilled and handsome. If children are to become clever and versatile in the use of their hands, they must have tools and materials to work with, a place to work, and "how to do it" books to refer to. One mother, in a small apartment, for weeks clambered over her son's pushmobile as it was being put together in the kitchen and counted her inconvenience well worth while.

DIFFERENCES BETWEEN BOYS' AND GIRLS' INTERESTS

Differences in play interests between boys and girls need more study. Up to about 8 or 9 interests seem to be fairly similar, but after that time there is less play involving both sexes.

But no boy is all "boy," any more than any girl is all "girl." There is a good deal of overlapping of so-called masculine and feminine traits in the sexes. This shows up early in such things as play interests, and later in preferences as to school subjects and vocational choices.

The generally known tendency toward superiority in males in such things as size, strength, and motor ability leads us to expect of boys the kinds of activities that go with these physical characteristics, and to expect different behavior in girls. Our social customs tend to encourage patterns of behavior in each sex that conform to our knowledge of physical differences. But it is important to keep in mind the mixture of femaleness and maleness in each child, and not to allow ourselves to have preconceived notions of what boys and girls are like.

The "tomboy" girl, who used to be disapproved of, is no longer frowned on; we recognize now that the value of lively activity and bodily freedom is as great for girls as for boys. For girls to play what used to be called "boys' games" encourages good feeling and understanding between the two sexes. But when an older girl seems to be making a protest against her feminine role in life by insisting on always wearing overalls, having a very short haircut, or turning up her nose at mixed parties, it should be a signal to us of the need of discovering why she is not following the more natural and usual course; for with the approach of puberty, most girls look forward to their feminine privileges of fripperies and cosmetics.

If her experiences with girls have not been happy, we must somehow fill in the gap between her interests and those of other girls. If she is trying to live up to what she thinks will please her father, who, having no son, calls her "my boy," and is proud of her masculine behavior, we must try to get him to see daylight. When sexual maturity is reached girls' play interests change very decidedly. Dolls are forgotten. In place of the earlier interests, whatever they were, comes an interest in parties and boys. Girls are maturing earlier than they used to, so parents should be prepared for their daughters' possible menstruation while they still tend to think of them as little girls. We can't, and don't want to, hold back growth, so we had better take in our stride the changes that make girls interested in boys, in movie stars, in lipstick—and in the privilege of shutting the family out of their room on occasion.

Girls quite often go through a time of wishing they were boys —few boys return the compliment. Mothers whose daughters grow up feeling that being a woman is a privilege thereby proclaim their own good adjustment. Some girls develop a belligerent feeling that the world is against women. There are inequalities, it is true. But if a girl has such a happy childhood that she never stops to think of wanting to be anyone but herself she is likely to be more contented in adult life than one who is full of protest.

TEAM PLAY

More and more, as children approach the teens, they enjoy organized team play. This means, of course, that they are becoming "socialized"; that they can think of the good of the group, and not merely of themselves. Earlier, they wanted to win personally; now having their "side" or team win looms large. Hockey, basketball, swimming, and football all give a chance for the development of this desirable spirit. Being exposed to physical pain, undergoing disappointment and, sometimes, unfair treatment are accepted as all a part of the game.

Children differ widely in the degree of their interest in group sports—or in sports at all, for that matter. A boy or girl who doesn't care much for team play is not necessarily a "poor

sport" on that account. He or she may be developing the same quality of being able to "take it" by competing with a single partner, as at tennis, or by pushing himself to the limit in high-jumping or on skis.

There is no reason for urging a child into something we think he *ought* to be interested in, provided he has enough variety in his play to be gaining from it physically, and isn't staying out of things on account of some hidden fear or feeling of inadequacy. Each child should be his own judge of what and how he wants to play—again provided he does not retreat from the everyday contacts that seem necessary to getting along with people. But it must not be forgotten that many children, left to their own devices, without a good example, are very limited and cramped in their interests. Parents and other adults can do a lot toward stimulating enjoyable interests by providing companionship and equipment.

WIDE OPPORTUNITIES FOR
GROWTH THROUGH PLAY

From the age of about 9 on, children engage in fewer different play activities. As they begin to have special interests, each thing that absorbs them will have to be given more time, so some things will drop out. Swimming, making a collection of butterflies, drawing cartoons—anything that becomes a hobby —will crowd out other forms of play.

This means that if we want children to have a rich, full life we will see to it that they have chances early for all sorts of experimentation. They are notorious for sudden enthusiasms, for scattering their energies over many activities that to adults often seem to have little or no value.

Back of these spurts of interest, many of which vanish as unexpectedly as they arise, is, of course, the child's intense curiosity and eagerness to learn about a great many different things. He wants to try things for himself, to explore, to experiment. He is no longer satisfied merely by pretending and imagining, he wants the real thing: the model plane a boy makes must really fly; the stove a girl cooks on must really bake.

In his craving for experience with the real, his "hunger for hard-pan," he comes to grief fairly often, or makes trouble. In her curiosity to see what will happen when the mercury in a thermometer reaches the top, Jean holds a lighted match under it. Tom wants to try out walking a plank 15 feet above the ground, and his mother suddenly looks out of the window to see him teetering on the beam of a new house next door.

Every mother can give dozens of illustrations of the folly and mischief this curiosity for real experience has led her children into. Fathers tend to take a lighter view: they don't have to clean up the mess as often, perhaps! They more often, too, take a longer view. Through having other interests, they have gained perspective, and are not quite so apt to be overanxious as mothers.

Nothing takes the place of real experiences, whether it be with mud (making dams), wind (flying kites), height (climbing trees), machinery (repairing a bicycle), stoves (cooking a meal), or paint (see Tom Sawyer).

All of these experiences should be as freely open to girls as to boys. Healthy comradeship now lays the foundation for future understanding. Douglas is not going to turn up his nose at Debbie as a "silly" girl because she plays with paper dolls if she also shares his passionate interest in raising puppies. Patty is not going to dismiss boys as "rough" if she has learned to admire and hold her own with them on the neighborhood baseball nine, or if Peter has helped her fly a kite.

Parents are often unnecessarily bothered because their children plunge into something hastily, only to drop it just as suddenly. This usually happens just about the time their father and mother have begun to take the new interest seriously. Jackie spends every spare minute wood carving with a paring knife, only to lose his enthusiasm by the time his father gets around to buying him a set of carving tools. Mildred is all excitement over tap dancing, but her interest peters out when Joan moves away and she has to go to take her lessons alone.

These are typical of situations that could be multiplied endlessly. The parent is disappointed because the child "doesn't stick to what he undertakes," especially if money and effort have been put into the project. The child is unable to say why his interest has melted away. Conflict results.

There are a number of things to be considered. First of all, perhaps the child has got what he wanted out of the experience. A child who has clamored for a chemistry set and who, after the first few weeks of feverish interest seems to have forgotten its existence may have got, in his added fame among the neighborhood boys, something of far greater value to him than further smelly experiments.

It is not to be expected that every path that entices a child will be followed to its end. In the course of exploring it, some more attractive bypath may open up. A girl who is in the seventh heaven over her chance to take part in a play may come to see that designing scenery is more to her liking. A boy who pleads for a printing press for the neighborhood gang's newspaper may wind up by being interested only in writing stories for it.

Childhood is a time for trying out many activities. Some of them will be only a flash in the pan. But what does that matter if the child is busy, interested, and learning? The variety of interests he has is even some measure of his intelligence.

Only intense curiosity is going to make it possible for children to persist and insist enough to explore a wide range of interests. Instead of being willing to take up the first leisure occupation at hand, such intelligent children are going to be all set to put their own ideas to work when they have spare moments.

"But," some thoughtful parents say, "Isn't it bad for a child not to finish what he sets out to do? Won't he learn habits of fickleness if he drifts from one thing to another? It's only by persevering, even if our enthusiasm has flagged, that we learn to be stable."

WHEN MUST A CHILD
STICK TO HIS LAST?

This is only partly true. Of course children must learn persistence at hard and sometimes uninteresting things. But don't their school work and home duties afford them plenty of practice in this? Perhaps in leisure time projects we ought not to limit them too much; we don't want them to lose interest in taking flyers in many kinds of ventures. Surely an adult needn't feel guilty if after taking up bowling as a hobby he decides it doesn't appeal to him, and tries golf instead. How are children with much less basis for judgment than adults, going to hit upon those things that are to have lasting interest unless they have chances to experiment and dabble?

An 8-year-old, fired by the skill of a friend, wants to take piano lessons. How can we tell without a few try-out lessons whether it is worth while to go on? If, after conscientious effort, a child who seems to lack the musical interest or dexterity of the hands necessary to real progress wants to stop, who can say that what she has learned hasn't been worth the time and money? If nothing else, she has learned to respect the musician, because she now has a notion as to the tremendous number of hours and concentrated effort that are back of good performance. She has also learned something about how to read music, and some musical terms that add to her vocabulary. Most important of all, she knows her own lack of interest in it and can move to something else.

A child who tends to scatter his energies so much that none of his efforts come to anything certainly needs help. One way of curbing such waste is to let the child feel the result of his too-hasty and short-lived enthusiasms, by bearing the expense himself. Such a plan works out better if based on an allowance. Jim's craze for collecting comic books suddenly vanishes in favor of making a glider. That the money he's been squandering would have gone a long way toward buying the materials for the glider will be all too evident even to Jim.

Letting a child learn by experience is very hard to do. From our vantage point we see farther ahead than can the child, so we tend to decide abruptly—"No, that's nonsense!" or "We know best," instead of letting the consequences of a child's decision come home, as it occasionally must, to roost.

WHY CHILDREN NEED PETS

Few of us look back on our childhood without tender memories of some pet. It may have been anything from a crow to a catamount, if you live in the country; if a city apartment cramped your style it may have had to be a canary, or a turtle that lived in a box.

To make it possible for a child to have close friendships with a living creature kindles sympathy and tenderness in the child. It also makes it possible for him to express affection without fear of embarrassment. A boy of 8 would be laughed at if he were always hugging his father or mother, but no one criticizes

the caresses he showers on his dog. Pets often show their love, and seldom, if at all, their disapproval. This is one of the great things a pet does for a child—it accepts him and doesn't find fault with him.

Finding suitable reading material about all those lovely, wiggly things that children bring home in cans and jars and pockets, should be our cue, instead of saying, "Don't bring that slimy thing into the kitchen!"

How much responsibility can and should children take for the care of pets? Parents are often disappointed because a child's fondness for animals doesn't make him invariably remember their needs. From 6 or so on a child can be entrusted with feeding a pet, and gradually with the other demands they make for care.

But they need reminding. Habits are established much easier in some children than others, and are of course set up faster when there are pleasant associations. But just as we may have to remind a boy to wash before coming to the table, even though we have encouraged this practice from early childhood, so we will probably have to remind him occasionally about feeding his goldfish, or putting out fresh water for his chickens. Let's make it reminding, though, not nagging.

Some parents hesitate to get their children pets because they remember the sorrow they felt when a pet died. This is not really a good reason; sooner or later every child comes up against death, and while we would not deliberately expose a child to grief, the benefits he gets from having close association with animals probably outweighs the shock when he has to part with them. Getting another dog or cat soon means that the new attachment will gradually dull the pain of loss. A child may protest that he will never feel the same about any other; but this merely means he doesn't know his capacity for love.

PETS AND SEX EDUCATION

Pets that have offspring do a lot of explaining. They illustrate better than pictures or words can how birth takes place, how mothers can care for their young. Instead of surrounding birth with mystery, as we so often do, we can bring it into the open through a mother dog or cat, and in the simplest, most natural way. The pig-tailed 8-year-old is ecstatic because the cat chose her bed to have her kittens on. Nine-year-old Peter gets up in the middle of the night to make sure the new puppies are all right. And lucky indeed are children on the farm, who intimately live with lambs, and baby chicks, and calves; who hear the coming events talked about in a casual, normal way.

And how better can the spiritual side of sex be shown than through the mother-love and parental care given young creatures? Even though a child doesn't have a pet that "belongs" to him, he can observe this in one of its most marked developments among birds.

But when they can, children should have that intimate understanding of animals that comes from living with them. We should think pretty carefully before we say "no" to a child's plea for a dog or a cat, or to his desire to raise rabbits.

SEX PLAY

Many a mother of 6- or 7-year-olds has been needlessly upset by finding that a group of neighborhood children has been carrying on sex play. Though of a quite innocent nature, probably such play has been secretly rather than openly engaged in because one of the children, at least, has had his natural curiosity about his body poorly handled, and thinks of such an interest as a forbidden one. We should not get panicky over such occurrences. As it is, the mothers involved often make something serious out of what should not be so regarded. In the present state of our ignorance and lack of understanding, there are almost always some mothers in a neighborhood who are so shocked that they withdraw their children from the group. This is unwise. Any action that causes children to feel guilty, or any punishment, should be avoided. It is often better to say nothing whatever to the children, for fear of saying too much, or the wrong thing. Instead, divert their minds, give them new interests. Get together and plan for more satisfying and constructive play activities. Often it falls to the lot of one or two women to take the responsibility for providing stimulating play materials, and a place for play.

To make such incidents stand out unhappily in a child's mind is exactly what we do not want to do. Wholesome attitudes toward sex are not built up by making a child feel that his interest in his body is something dirty or bad.

6

Home life as preparation of independent living

In our thinking and in our planning for children, we should keep in mind two facts: That each child is an individual, and should be treated as one; and that he will always have to live with other individuals, with whose needs and desires he must harmonize his own.

Every child is unique in temperament, intelligence, and physical make-up. He's unlike anyone else in the world, even in his own family, and his home should be the place above all others where his needs, springing from his individual differences, will be sympathetically appreciated. This is the place that cam be counted on to understand the slow-moving child, the one who bubbles with laughter at wrong moments, the impulsive one who makes awkward mistakes. Unless each member is dignified by being given this special understanding, the family fails in one of its reasons for being. This cherishing of the qualities that make a child stand out—such as a lovably generous nature, or striking originality—is a function of the home. In the home, too, there is forgiveness for irritable flare-ups caused by strains and tensions endured outside. Here a child is known intimately enough so that his moody silence or his excited chattering is interpreted in terms of what has been happening to him.

But just as important as being sympathetically understood is each child's obligation to contribute to the life of his home. He has to learn to be a giver as well as a taker. When a child's parents give him real practice in cooperation in this small-scale world of his home he will be equipped to fit into the always broadening life he becomes a part of as he grows older.

CHILDREN'S NEEDS AS INDIVIDUALS

It is amazing to think of the endless number of different combinations of traits that can occur in human beings. No matter how many children a family has, no two are alike. Each displays characteristics of mind, of emotion, of social and other tendencies that are as original as his appearance. Two brothers may have "their father's nose" but they won't have exactly the same kind of chin, or ears, or mind, or emotional make-up; for the genes meeting in each of them come from a great number of ancestors, from any one of whom it would be possible to inherit only a very limited number of characteristics.

This helps us realize that the needs of two children are never exactly alike. From food to more subtle needs, we must expect and prepare for different wants.

Even in infancy, children show marked personality differences, in degree of timidity or aggression, activity, irritability, and responsiveness. By school age we must expect that there will be even greater differences. Some of the strikingly individual behavior of infancy will have lessened, some will have become more pronounced. The little girl who has a gentle, motherly attitude will probably not lose this quality; it may be shown in a generally helpful attitude toward those she plays with. Another child, rather violently self-assertive from the start, may, through having lots of experience with other children, tone down her noisy demands as she comes to see she gets along much better by being tactful.

Sometimes a child is a sort of "ugly duckling" for a while, hard to understand, showing interests that are far afield from his parents', or a very different kind of temperament. An extremely quiet child may show up at a loss in a noisy, lively family; a child who has a marked sense of humor behind a grave, serious face, or who is deeply sensitive under seeming coldness, may be misunderstood by his family. Children who are blunt, children whose minds move so quickly it's hard to keep up with them, or children who are slow, may be set down in families unprepared to handle them.

Grandparents can be lifesavers of children who are so puzzling their parents find it hard to accept them.

CHILDHOOD IS WORTHY OF RESPECT

Then there is a more general reason for individualizing our treatment of children; that childhood itself is worthy of respect. No child is in a position to hold his own in an adult world. We need to be very careful not to take advantage of children's smaller size and limited experience.

In the past it was assumed that adults must be respected, regardless of whether or not they were really "grownups" emotionally. By degrees we have come to see that children's opinions and ideas should be sought and given consideration. This builds a mutual feeling of trust. Scoldings without asking why things happened, spankings that take advantage of adult size and strength, accepting invitations for children without consulting them first, and opening their letters are some of the ways in which parents sometimes show disrespect for their children. Because we get used to safeguarding and protecting children while they are small and helpless we may grow to act with more rather than less authority as time goes on, As our children develop and begin to stand on their own feet we must do some careful planning in order to give over more and more control of their actions to them. Letting them make more decisions, even if they sometimes make poor ones, is about the only way parents can provide against the time when their children will have to manage their own lives.

WHAT CAN FAMILYLIFE CONTRIBUTE?

When we ask ourselves, "What is the purpose of family life?" we can see that it is much more than giving love and physical care to our children. In preparing them for independent living we have the responsibility, also, of handing down to them from the past, ways and customs that have been found to be good.

All peoples, in all ages, have had special traditions. They range all the way from methods used in training children to those that grow up around the planting of crops or the ways of building houses. Some of these are valuable, others of less importance, like table manners. In ancient Greece, for example, custom ruled that children must learn to hold their bread in their left hand, other foods in their right. Our children, for several hundred years, have been taught to eat with spoons and forks.

These are merely surface customs. They don't deal with matters that go deep. But there are customs that encourage the stability of family life and that deserve to be passed on to our children. The family celebration of anniversaries and holidays, and certain traditions of a region, country, or religion are examples. We prize our memories of special family ways of observing Christmas and birthdays—the precious tree ornaments brought out from their tissue-paper wrappings year after year, the ceremony of the candle-decked cake. Such time-honored customs bring a family together, and deepen the relationships between its members. When we Americans work hard so that we can own our own homes, we are showing that we cherish the ideal of warmth and strength and permanence in family life. It is one way we demonstrate the solid and lasting qualities of family relationships that we want to emphasize for our children.

As time goes on, and new inventions and added knowledge bring about changed ways of living, we must keep looking at our traditional customs, to see if they fit in with the new conditions. We parents are not always conscious of our role as interpreters of the values in our ways of life. Only by examining them carefully can we see which are really valuable, and which we go through the motions of preserving only because we are used to them. No mother would think of wearing hoop skirts such as our ancestors wore, to do her housework; when we cling to ideas that are no more valuable than old-fashioned clothes, we may be hampering our progress.

Because of our natural tendency to hang onto the kind of home and family life in which we grew up, we need to welcome and accept new ways when they are improvements on the old.

Some ways of life ring true eternally. Kindness, loyalty, honesty shine through the customs that grow out of these ways. Sometimes customs reflect change for the better. In pioneer days, when the father was the physical protector of the family as well as the breadwinner it was often necessary for him to have strict authority over the lives of his family. How long it takes for us to recognize changes in custom is illustrated by the pain and confusion that sometimes result when a father's "say-so" is still considered much more important than a mother's, although she, as well as he, may be earning a part of the family income, and may have quite as sound judgment as he about child guidance. We get very mixed up and don't quite know how to take social change. When women pout because men no longer give up their seats to them in buses they forget that they forfeited that kind of gallantry when they began to compete wit& men for jobs.

Sensible parents, then, will keep alert to the need of living in the present. We need to look much more to the future than to the past when it comes to thinking of what we want our children to carry on as a precious heritage of family life.

Families provide practice in democratic living. One thing we can be sure will be useful to our children is a democratic way of life in their homes. If the future of the world is to become brighter we must practice mutual understanding and helpfulness among nations, in the hope of real world brotherhood.

The home demonstrates democratic living in terms that a child can understand. Here he can have daily lessons in sharing responsibilities, as well as fun, food, clothes, and love. Even if his share in family matters is at first very small, he begins to get the idea; he has a voice in deciding where to go for a picnic, or what color the house is to be painted. And he listens in his turn.

Children's sharing of responsibility is taken for granted; but do they always get something out of it? The parents' attitude makes all the difference. One little girl exploded one day, saying, "It's this *helping* that I don't like! I wish I could ever be given something to do by myself. If I had a job to do that I could do *my own way* I wouldn't mind working."

Few children express their feelings as well as this; but if we would put ourselves in our children's places once in a while we might be surprised at how tired we'd get of being always on tap to run errands or to do the less interesting parts of jobs. What if we were hardly ever consulted as to what our ideas were—or were snubbed for having any? "You aren't I, so how can you know what I'd like?" questioned one child.

Just as a girl gets to be more careful of her shoes when she must buy them out of her allowance, so with any learning experience. To be responsible, a child must have a stake in, must see the reason for, what he's asked to do. When parents take the trouble to try to understand what children see as important, things go better. It's so easy for us adults to see the reason back of what we want a child to do or learn, and be forgetful of the fact that he's too immature to be interested.

Boys of 9 or 10, for example, are pretty indifferent to cleanliness. Oh, on occasion they will get themselves up spick and span. But then it's usually because they think mother will be pleased, and let them go to the movie (if that's in the front of their minds at the moment). We'd be uneasy if they *were* very much concerned about keeping clean. It's so unlike boy nature we might even look around for a psychiatrist to reassure us!

Our problem, then, if we want Gordie to come to the table with clean hands is: how to make him *interested* in washing, not how to *make* him do it. (Any adult, being bigger and stronger, can *make* a child do things—at what cost to both!)

WHY REMINDING IS NECESSARY

This matter of the gap between our ideas as to things that seem important, and our children's ideas, should make us realize how easy it is for children to forget. Ten-year-old Lora doesn't need to be reminded to read the funnies. Why does she have to be reminded not to leave the newspaper strewn over the floor?

We might as well resign ourselves to the need of reminding our children about a great many of their responsibilities long after it *seems* to us that "they ought to be able to remember." With all the many interests they have to explore, how can they keep their minds on the exact things we want them to remember?

But let's *keep* it reminding. Jogging a child's memory in a pleasant way brings better results than nagging at him. (Who can say that much surface friction in marriage may not date back to little boys' distaste for their mothers' harping, sometimes with rasping voices, on relatively unimportant matters? Does a man sometimes confuse his wife's voice with that of his mother, and resist being made a "little-boy" culprit?) Maybe when a child says "I didn't hear you" it's because he has unconsciously learned to turn a deaf ear to the mosquito-buzz of our everlasting, droning criticism.

Another way of assuring that children are with us rather than against us is to make our directions clear and simple. Lots of times children really don't understand what we want because we use too many words.

Also, children of these ages are so *busy* they are entitled to a warning ahead of time. "There's just time for you to finish that game before doing the dishes."

To know that it isn't only *our* children that seem so heedless and forgetful helps, too. Sometimes all a mother needs to give her a lift is the reassurance of learning she's not "a failure" at bringing about good habits; that the willing compliance of her children when she does remind them is in itself a good habit.

And why not praise children more when they do remember?

Sharp words about tracks on the kitchen floor can't be wiped out the way the mud can. *We* need to be reminded that praise is a very strong stimulant to good behavior.

If we are clever when we are faced with this problem of getting cooperation instead of mere results we'll put our thinking on what we want our child to get out of it rather than on what *we* get out of it. We are pleased when a child is obedient and docile. But we should make sure that this is not mere obedience to *us*. What we want to bring about is obedience, or allegiance, to sound principles of behavior.

PERSONAL RESPONSIBILITY

Between the ages of 6 and 12 a child can assume more and more responsibility about the care of his person. With a little reminding he can take care, before the end of this period, of such things as baths, changes of underwear, selection of what to wear from day to day, and of putting his clothes in the laundry. Depending on the opportunity and kind of instruction a child has, he or she should be able to do such things as washing out socks or shorts, doing a fair job of simple ironing, sewing on buttons, and the like. Deciding about haircuts, remembering about feeding and watering the chickens and bringing in the eggs, planning ahead to have a clean dress or shirt saved for a special occasion are the kinds of things for which children should gradually assume responsibility.

Giving older boys and girls responsibility for younger brothers and sisters has to be very thoughtfully considered. Mary, at 11, may be mature enough to take 6-year-old Joe to and from school on the bus, but it may take some explaining to get her to see **that** this does not give her the right to tell him how much sugar he can put on his cereal!

RESPONSIBILITY FOR HOUSEHOLD TASKS

Boys and girls, if they are to be prepared for their own family life later, need to become familiar with the details of family routines. By the time they are 12 they should be putting up their own lunches, doing simple cooking, planning and carrying out projects like cleaning their own rooms.

Children who live on farms have an advantage over city children. They may have first-hand experience in work by means of which millions of people earn their living. They care for stock, or even raise them, learn to use and repair machinery, and help get meals for threshers. The city boy's job of washing the family car, and his sister's practice in helping to serve at church suppers are examples of the less frequent work opportunities coming to urban children.

City or country, parents have a challenge to meet in providing experiences that will help their children become self-reliant and useful. To find the happy medium between the overburdening with back-breaking farm chores or early morning newspaper route that have made many men hate the memory of their boyhood and the too-soft life which many families are tempted to provide isn't easy.

One of the things we parents may not give much thought to is how our attitude toward work affects our children. Our groans, or the enthusiasm with which we attack a job, are not lost on them. If mother has to beg father to put on the screens, or if she is forever moaning about the way dirty dishes pile up three times a day, is it to be wondered at that John and Jane think of those two jobs as something to be avoided?

Of course few of us go at all the humdrum chores that we have to do with bursting enthusiasm. But the very fact that people have such different attitudes toward routine tasks proves that such things can be enjoyable, or disagreeable, depending on our training. Why does one woman like to cook, and another hate it? Does it hark back in part to childhood experience? Did the mother of the former let her daughter experiment, and praise her on the outcome? A woman who neglects her house in favor of her flower beds may have had a mother who disliked housework herself, and made it seem a dreary business. Or, she may have been so expert at it that she couldn't be bothered with teaching her daughter.

To see how hard anyone, child or grown-up, will work at something he likes to do should give us a tip. What immense effort children put into collecting for a paper sale, painting a bicycle, making cookies for a Girl Scout party! Why not make sure that our children enjoy many kinds of work by seeing that the conditions under which they learn are pleasant—like singing, or saying funny verses while the dishes are being washed.

Working with children is one way to do it. Any mother of a 10-year-old knows how much longer he or she will stick at a job, how much more she can "get out of him if she works alongside—raking leaves, piling wood, washing windows, or the inevitable daily dishes. To the objection that this takes almost as much time as doing the job oneself there is an unanswerable argument. We are developing long-time attitudes in our children and having companionship with them, too.

One of our great temptations as parents is to neglect letting children have experience in being helpful around the house because it's easier to do things ourselves. It could become a matter of pride with us to seize many more opportunities than we do to give children this practice.

It is generally believed that one of the most powerful preventives of juvenile delinquency is to give children the happiness of feeling that they are useful members of society. To contribute to the family community is the first step.

In a former day, many children probably had to do too much, too early in life. No one would want to go back to the time when on farms or in factories children labored long hours, beyond their strength. But in modern life, many children take their first steps into mischief because they are at loose ends. No one takes the trouble to see that they have the satisfaction that comes from having a part, a really meaningful part, in the busy life around them.

7

Helping children to make the most of their mental ability

All of us hope our children will be bright. To us, they always seem wonderful, but we are so close to them that we aren't very good judges of their ability.

Before children have gone to school very long we begin to get an idea as to how their minds compare with those of other children. The school's estimate of Janet's ability will keep us from pushing her, if she has only a fairly able mind; when we are told that Jim is mentally advanced we will try to provide special opportunities for him.

In considering a child's school progress his mental level is not the only thing that has to be thought of. Suppose Mark has trouble keeping up with his classmates. Is it inability to grasp the work that is holding him back, or is something disturbing him emotionally?

No amount of help or prodding will cause a slow child to become a genius. But by recognizing his real capacity we can protect his happiness and self-respect by not nagging at him. If, by chance, it is the school, not we, that expects too much of him, we can help out. We can explain, perhaps, that while John is slow, he's a sticker, and so conscientious that care must be taken not to worry him.

Finding out what we can about a child's mental ability is necessary in making plans for his education, and for later vocational guidance.

WHAT IS INTELLIGENCE?

It is hard to define intelligence; no psychologist ever seems quite satisfied with another's definition, let alone his own. But the kind of intelligence measured by mental tests may be described as an individual's ability to grasp problems, to invent ways of meeting them, and to criticize his ways of working out solutions. In other words, a person is intelligent to the degree that he adapts himself to new conditions, and has a planned goal toward which he is working. Ted shows intelligence when he telephones home for the name of a store whose address he has lost. June uses her mind under new conditions when she hunts for a vegetable to take the place of the one her mother sent her to buy, but which the store is out of.

Such an interpretation of intelligence is narrow; it leaves out certain kinds of inborn capacities such as musical ability, and mechanical aptitudes seen in cleverness in dealing with things. Such a definition does not bring into the picture all that a child's personality embraces—the amount of drive or ambition he has, his attitudes, aspirations, and (to some degree) his imagination.

There is unevenness in ability, and there are also clusters of abilities that seem to be grouped at random. One child may be higher in mechanical ability than in language skills. Another may be a nimbler with his hands, but adept in using words. Artistic ability is so marked in Jim that his lack of a particularly high I. Q. goes unnoticed. In Dick's case, it is obvious that while he rates very high on mental tests, he is surprisingly short on common sense.

However, the value of our present intelligence tests is considerable in connection with a child's progress at school; they do tell us something about the kinds of work and interests lie can fruitfully pursue.

WHAT CONTRIBUTIONS CAN PARENTS MAKE?

We cannot *make* our children live up in accomplishment to whatever intelligence they may have. But we can supply surroundings that stimulate them, try to keep their aspirations high, and show our appreciation of their efforts. These are some of the concrete ways we can help:

1. We can offer our children many chances to have practice in attacking problems that call upon their ingenuity and in itiative. Such children are learning to think and reason. These are abilities school work calls on increasingly as children pro gress through the grades.

A child of 6 does not "reason" it out for himself that his shoes will get dirty if he plays in a mud puddle. But the responsibility for cleaning his own shoes will help him to make the connection.

Children love to discuss causes, and the reasons for things. Families can have fun exploring questions that come up; and ingenious parents will find ways of setting children to work searching out answers.

The more dealings a child has with materials and objects, the more readily he can put facts together and reason out relationships, causes, and effects. Does he find the answers to such questions as why some wood splits when you drive nails in it, or when is a screw better than a nail? The little girl who is allowed to get meals by herself reasons out that she had better put the potatoes in to bake first, once she has had the disappointment of finding them still almost raw when the rest of the meal was ready. At every turn learning by *doing* encourages the use of the mind. Learning from a book how long it takes potatoes to bake will not make the forceful impression that experience does.

2. We can greatly enrich and stimulate children by providing surroundings in which they will have not only freedom to ex plore, but materials to experiment with and learn from. Many families have a hard time doing this, because they are so cramped

for space—no attic, no basement, no place where children can work on puppets, or keep their aquarium.

We must make it possible for children to carry out the things their eager curiosity pushes them into doing whether with tools, clay, paints, needles and thread, or a printing outfit. If such resources aren't provided, we mustn't be surprised if they turn to commercially supplied amusements to find excitement. Do those who deplore the stacks of comic books under their children's beds provide a place where more creative experiences can be indulged? We all consider a kitchen, where food for children's bodies is prepared, essential. Is a workshop where food for mental growth can be supplied any less important?

Reading aloud in the family circle is tops as a way of stimulating mental activity, and it is one pleasure that no family need be without. Those who have public libraries in their community could make better use of them. Those who don't could work for better county and traveling library service.

Few of us can afford as many books and magazines as we would like to provide. Perhaps having a special book fund would remind us to make better use of the dollar spent for amusement or a kitchen gadget we don't actually need.

A good children's encyclopedia is one of the most valuable things a family can invest in. Even before they can read, children's eagerness for information results in their absorbing much knowledge through pictures.

When so many good reprints are to be found in 25-cent and $1 editions, there is little excuse for failing to have good reading available. From the time children hear the old familiar nursery rhymes their parents were brought up on, reading aloud is a springboard to learning. Families that have laughed over the "Just So" or "Rootabaga" stories with their 6-year-olds will still be having jolly hours together reading "Mutiny on the Bounty" or "The Yearling" when the children are entering the teens. What a lot of history, biology, astronomy, and the like will have been eagerly absorbed by the unsuspecting listeners!

Reading aloud in the family circle enriches children's minds and furnishes a basis for stimulating conversation. By discussing what we read we encourage children to examine many sides of a question before accepting or rejecting it. Young children are prone to believe what they see in print, so it is well worth while

for parents to talk about current events that are written up in the news, or argued about in forum discussions on the radio.

3. Not only can parents share with their children the pleasure and profit to be had from good books, but they also can share with them in creative activities that lead to satisfying skills. Families that do things with their hands encourage the centering **of** activities at home. In addition they give their children a chance to take part in exciting forms of self-expression like weaving, pottery making, wood or soap carving, painting, photog raphy, and other hobbies.

Excursions, whether in town or country, to see a bakery, or dairy, to explore a quarry or sand pit, or to visit the docks or the railroad yards which teem with goods from far places, are experiences that cost little beyond the time involved, and they make children's imaginations soar.

Both creative activities and adventures with their parents stimulate children to get more information from books, and so are particularly desirable in cases where a child would be able to do his school work better if he read more.

4. Parents should discriminate between encouraging their children's belief in their own powers, and stimulating an arro gantly aggressive competitive spirit. Competition plays a big

part in our way of life, but it is only after children are old enough to go to school that they show much in the way of competitive spirit. Once they are part of a large group they are often faced with the temptation to try to outdo others or with the fear of being outdone by them. Even though the school may conscientiously try to measure each one's achievement in terms of his past performance, there are all sorts of other ways in which children are compared with one another. There is a prize for the child turning in the largest amount of waste paper; a child who learns all his spelling words early in the week is excused from that class on Thursday and Friday; John excels at swimming, Ted at pitching a ball.

How much parents influence a child's competitive spirit no one knows; but it is safe to say that there are at least two distinct and obvious directions this influence may take. Parents who are intensely ambitious for themselves and for their child may arouse a strong consciousness of the competitive nature of many of our activities. "We must have our house painted! It looks so shabby now that the Abbotts have restuccoed theirs!" Or, "Joe got a raise and he's not half as smart as you are." The ideas back of such remarks sink in, and become a part of the children's way of thinking.

Having a father who is so bent on improving himself that he goes to night school, or a mother who does the laundry in order to save money to buy good phonograph records may mean to the children merely "keeping up with the Joneses'* or it may mean that they have a vision of the inner satisfactions that come to their parents from such efforts.

Our goal is to interest the child in enjoying a job well done, and getting pleasure out of his contribution, not out of beating the other fellows.

5. Above all, we can contribute to our children's best use of their mental powers by accepting them as they are, and expecting of them only what it is possible for them to achieve. It is not the amount of brains a child has but how harmoniously his mind and his emotions work together to help him to fit into the social scheme that counts.

8

When home and school get together

Offhand most of us would probably say that we send our children to school to get an education. But do we really know what we mean by an education? Do we think of it as reading, writing, geography, music, and history, something confined to the school building, or do we think of education as a process that has been going on ever since the child was born, and that will continue all his life?

If we consider it in this larger way it is an exciting thing to have a hand in. No matter how active we have been in a child's informal education at home, we all lean heavily on the help of the school, where his more formal learning will take place. Some parents seem to wash their hands of all responsibility once they have waved their children good-by at the school door; but more thoughtful ones want to know what's happening in the school, what the aims of educators are, and how they can help their children get all they can out of their school experience.

Dividing the school day into subjects to which 20 or 40 minutes are assigned is of little help to a child's understanding of how to get along with people, or of assuring him happy learning experiences. School is life, nowadays, and the education that a child is getting at home is an inseparable part of that life. As subject matter boundaries are broken down, so the dividing line between home and school should be broken, too.

DO YOU KNOW YOUR CHILD'S SCHOOL?

Parents certainly can't content themselves with hustling their children off in the morning, rested, well-fed, and clean. They've got to go along with them in spirit, every day; and in person often enough to learn how they can reinforce what the school is doing. Younger school-age children love to have their parents visit school, yet some parents never put their heads inside the school door unless they are sent for because their child *is* in trouble.

What are some of the things parents gain by school visits?

1. Even a very limited acquaintance with a child's teacher helps to throw light on his behavior in school, and it is an ad vantage to his teacher to get a glimpse of what the child's family and home life are like—which she can get some notion of even in a brief talk with his mother or father.

2. By visiting the schoolroom we get a chance to see our child in relation to others. We sense something of how he is accepted by the group; whether the behavior we have noticed at home is common among children of this age; and why he either likes or dislikes school.

3. For his parents to demonstrate their interest by taking the time to visit school, to go to parent-teacher meetings or open house, bolsters up a child's feeling of the importance of school. How can we expect children to keep on having the glowing belief that school is a wonderful place—almost invariably their attitude when they start out—if we groan and grumble over giving only one night a month to school affairs? By our attitude we do a great deal to prompt our children's. "Timothy just hates school, and I don't blame him. I always felt that way myself," says Tim's mother—in his hearing, too. She has never taken the trouble to see whether there's really something hateful about the school, or whether he's echoing her because he thinks it's the

thing to do. Tim's school may be as good as his mother's was poor, but he is not getting the support he needs at home.

4. Parents may find by keeping in touch with school that they can very capably supplement what goes on there. Hearing a social-studies discussion may remind Mrs. White of a map or pictures that she can send to school by Jack. Or discussion of a certain locality may bring up the question in the family, "Why don't we drive there some Sunday, and learn more about it?" Parents need to be on the alert to foster children's interests and abilities, any one of which may have an influence on vocational choice.

Parents can be used in schools, too. They can work in the lunchroom, help on projects, display their hobbies, and arrange for reading rooms and parents' meetings there.

5. Parents need to visit school to break down the barriers that sometimes exist between them and the teacher.

A good many parents are afraid of teachers. They feel that teachers will be contemptuous of them because they are not so well educated, and can't talk the teacher's language. They can't talk the plumber's or the electrician's language, either. All of us have our special fields of knowledge, and it's absurd to be standoffish with each other. Sometimes teachers are even more afraid of parents, because they get so much criticism from them. They tremble at the thought of home visits, especially at the beginning of their career. And often, teachers thoughtlessly blame parents for things they don't understand, things that can be remedied by mutual respect and trust.

Instead of being suspicious and fearful parents and teachers need to get together. It should be easy when they have the common ground of interest in children to stand on. The trend nowadays toward replacing report cards by individual conferences with parents should do a lot toward bringing together the two institutions that are the most powerful influences in children's lives.

Schools have changed so much in the last few years that even comparatively young parents should be very careful not to criticize a child's school on the basis of their own experience. Even though we are not able to understand what the school is trying to accomplish by a certain procedure, we had better withhold our judgment until we can find out. Parents weaken a child's morale when they divide his allegiance by scoffing at things the school is trying to do. The school needs our backing.

If we are really convinced, after study, that something is wrong, we can voice our opinion through an organization set up to serve our needs, such as the parent-teacher association. This is a much more effective way of bringing about changes than by acting individually.

To "take sides" with a child against his teacher, or some school rule, without getting the facts is to undermine the school's authority unfairly. Naturally parents feel protective toward their children. But there is a difference between the hasty, violent reaction that we all feel when we imagine our "young" are threatened, and the more mature approach that refuses to let blind mother- or father-love or pride get in the way of a sensible study of the question involved. Whether it's a matter of believing that Pat is being bullied on the playground; that Irene isn't being taught to read soon enough; or that Marcia's report of her teacher's sarcasm is true, a calm approach rather than an immediate taking of the child's part will give better results—and save us from possible shame-facedness, later.

We are unreasonable if we expect the teachers to whom we entrust our children to be superior human beings, unless at the same time we pay them adequately. We ought to make sure that people of good ability will enter this field. When we hand over to schools and teachers the most precious things in the world to us—our children—we ought to do everything possible to provide emotionally mature, broadminded, intelligent, and alert teachers who are capable of taking on one of the biggest jobs in the world today.

In many communities, teachers are bound by rules of behavior parents wouldn't want imposed on themselves. Often a teacher is expected to *devote her spare time to supervising clubs or other activities. In many places there is still discrimination against married teachers, whose experience with children of their own may give them sympathetic insight into other children's needs. A teacher should be allowed to be a real person.

One of the matters parents often need to talk over with the school is that of promotions. Most children move along from grade to grade in the group they entered school with. A great many schools now automatically "pass" all children in the lower grades. But there are many circumstances such as prolonged absence due to illness, or irregularity for some other cause, which make it best for a child to repeat a grade. It is far better for a child to do this than it is for him to go on and hopelessly flounder later because of poor preparation, or immaturity in relation to his group.

Occasionally a child finds his class work so easy that he Is not challenged to work up to his capacity. Schools used to promote such a child to a higher grade. This sometimes resulted in his being thrown in with children who were physically larger and more able. In order not to create this second problem schools now usually attempt to enrich his experience at the more suitable grade level. Giving him special projects or letting him read when the class is busy with things in which he does not need day-to-day practice sometimes eases the situation. Often parents can be of great assistance in giving such a child stimulating outside interests that will keep him on his toes. Music, handicrafts, or classes at a good art school may be better ways of encouraging in him habits of application and effort than urging that he be pushed ahead a grade at school. Being free to visit the library, to go on trips with his father, or to take advantage of other ways of using his abilities is exhilarating to a child of superior mental gifts.

Whatever the problem, the interests of the child will be best served only when his home and school get together on a plan for solving it.

LEARNING TO READ AND WRITE

To most of us, going to school means, first of all, learning to read. And this skill is, perhaps, the most important single one a child has to acquire, for without a firm grasp of reading he is helpless when he comes up against other things he wants to know about.

Because parents recognize how very closely the ability to read ties up with their child's school progress they often try to help him get a start before he goes to school. Odd as it seems, these efforts sometimes hinder him more than they help him. Direct teaching of the alphabet at home, for example, is unnecessary; but it will be very helpful indeed if a child is given plenty of experience in solving his own problems. For the business of learning to read is full of problems, from learning to recognize the "shape" of different words, and concentrating on one's "place" on the page, to meeting the competition of someone quicker than oneself. It matters very little whether a child is able to print his name when he goes to school (though many 5-year-olds do pick this up), but it is a great advantage if he has been read to and talked with a lot, so that he understands what many words mean, and can connect them with experiences he has had and explanations he has been given.

Parents should let their children lead the way in any before-school reading practice. Many a bright child gets a good start at reading from signs, headlines, and advertisements. But it serves no good purpose to *urge* the printed word on children before they go to school.

Another thing that matters is that a child shall be *ready* to learn to read. This does not suddenly become true just because he becomes 6 years old. Some children will be ready earlier, some much later. A child's mental age counts much more than his calendar age in years. Some of the children in a first-grade room will be all set to go ahead quickly, others will need a much more gradual approach.

The teacher must be alert to see the different needs of different children, some of whom will demand much more of her time and effort than others. If individual workbooks are provided for the children to use, she may be able to put her finger on the special difficulties of any certain child. With such materials, the one who catches on quickly can go ahead at his own rate of speed; the teacher can spend more of her time on those who need more help. Parents' interest in cooperating with the teacher is far more important than any coaching they may give their child, for few of them are familiar with the highly developed techniques the teacher uses in opening up the world of books to children.

Some parents do not realize the tremendous advantage with which a child starts out if he has a good first-grade teacher. When he is taking his first steps in school adjustment and his future habits of learning, it is vital that his teacher be well-trained. Great numbers of children are not only slowed down by a poor start, but more or less permanent damage is done to their self-esteem and confidence in their ability in general.

They may acquire feelings of timidity and self-distrust that are very hard indeed to shake off. One child, although slow to start in reading, may pick up fast at 7, 8, or 9. Another may find reading hard for a long time. Each child needs to be allowed to travel at his own pace.

HOW PARENTS CAN HELP

Parents cannot themselves determine whether their 6-year-old is ready for first grade, but they can do much to prepare him for reading experience. Their pleasantly stimulating companionship is far more important to a child than being taught any particular skill.

Poised, happy children attack any new adventure with more spirit than children who have worries and fears; so those parents who have succeeded in keeping their children easy and relaxed can feel they have taken a long step toward preparing them for *all* their school experiences. Children who already know how to play with other children will not find it hard to work with them. Having an orderly life at home, and doing things in a regular and systematic way, will help them to fit into the routine that has to be observed at school. Joe, who has learned to dress himself without help, who is accustomed to coming to meals when he is called, will find taking responsibility at school natural. Ray, who has always had attention at home the moment he demanded it, will find it harder to settle down to work at school without constantly seeking help from the teacher than Kenneth, whose parents have taught him not to interrupt them rudely with clamorous demands.

Another way of getting children ready for learning to read goes on quietly and pleasurably in some homes from the time

they learn to talk. In such homes interesting and varied experiences, like trips to the zoo, or to farms, are almost as much a part of the children's life as eating and sleeping. Picture and story books have whetted their curiosity and imagination. Parents have taken their questions seriously.

Fathers and mothers who take pains to show their children how to recognize different kinds of trees or insects; to explain to them things like where coal, wood, butter, paper, or bread come from, will be rewarded not only by their children's having a wide general fund of information but also by their ability to listen attentively. This will be very useful to them when in school they have to listen to, remember, and follow directions. Giving children a chance to express their observations and imaginings fosters clear thinking. Encouraging them to tell about their experiences will help them talk before an audience, a matter of growing importance at school.

If jingles and rhymes and games involving word sounds and meanings have been a part of the child's play experience at home he will have an interest in words that will help him in learning to read. Hearing clear and correct pronunciation rather than the slovenly speech we all fall into so easily will help children to recognize words when they meet them in print. It's all very well to be amused by a 3-year-old's calling "window" "windle" or "basket" "bastick," but it is unfair to him to let him enter school with such mispronunciations.

Finally, readiness for reading means *interest* in learning to read. A child who has been introduced to the world about him by means of trips and excursions, who has heard many stories and has had access to picture books, who appreciates something of how reading will be the "open, sesame" that will unlock a whole new wonderful world to him, will look forward to learning to read with eagerness and enjoyment.

READING DIFFICULTIES

If a child has trouble learning to read, there are several explanations that may not occur at once to his parents. The sooner the difficulty is located the better.

A child's eyesight is among the first things to think of. School tests of children's eyes often pick up only very noticeable defects, so they cannot be relied on completely. Whether a child needs glasses or not should be determined by a competent eye specialist.

Sometimes difficulty in learning to read can be traced to poor hearing. A child who does not hear clearly will have trouble with reading. What he hears and the words for which it stands may have no relation. If the loss of hearing is serious, the child may need to be placed in a special class. If the loss is very slight, having a seat near the teacher may be all that is needed to avoid difficulty in learning to read. (See pp. 186, 187.)

Does handedness enter in?

A good many children go through a period of confusion before they learn to read from left to right across the page. A child's experience in following the comic strips may help him a bit to gain this sense of direction, which should make parents less impatient about reading them to him. For the left-handed child a right-to-left direction is the natural one. When such a child is given paper to write or draw on, it should be placed on a slant opposite to that in which right-handed people place paper. If this is not done, the left-handed child will be forced to twist his wrist around and write or draw in an awkward, back-handed way.

Long before children go to school their handedness has been established. No attempt should be made either by parents or teacher to force a left-handed child to write with his right hand.

Children who are just starting to learn to read often reverse letters and words; that is, they confuse "b's" and "d's," read "saw" for "was," and write letters and figures backwards. When this confusion persists beyond what seem natural limits, that is, when a child does not gradually "see" words and letters as they are, he will need patient individual help if he is not to become discouraged.

Is he a happy child?

Few parents realize that a child's slowness in learning to read may have little or nothing to do with reading itself. Instead it may be the result of an unhappy frame of mind that interferes with his giving close attention to his reading. The first adult relationship he enters into outside his home is usually with his teacher, who takes the place of his mother while he *is* at school. If he has done things willingly and gladly for his mother, the chances are he will try hard to do what the teacher wants him to. But if he is not on good terms with his mother, this attitude may be transferred to his teacher, and he will not make any effort to learn to read.

When a child is sullen and resistant about reading, when he refuses to put forth the necessary effort, we are apt to think this results from his struggles with reading. Actually, it may be the other way round; his difficulty with reading may come from his inability to get rid of some burden he carries which keeps him from entering into a cooperative relationship with his teacher. Perhaps the child's and the teacher's dispositions may clash. Teachers, like parents and everybody else, may have problems of personality, of family life, that handicap them in their relations with children.

When emotional problems resist the earnest efforts of teachers and parents alike, the help of mental-health experts should be sought. If there is no local child-guidance clinic, the State Department of Education will know where such services may be found.

The fact that more boys than girls have trouble learning to read suggests the possibility that there may be less understanding of boys' needs than of girls' on the part of mothers; that women are too apt to demand behavior of their sons that fits into their own scheme of life. Because girls are not naturally quite so aggressive as boys, they may find conformance easier. In this connection, too, it should be remembered that girls are slightly ahead in their general development, and for this reason they may find learning to read easier than boys do.

Certainly a child's emotional resistance toward reading must not be dismissed with the easy, surface explanation that it is a result of his finding reading hard. The reason reading is the thing around which emotional attitudes grow up is probably because it is so much stressed in the early grades, and so much prized by parents as evidence of a child's brightness.

Once a child has developed a feeling of hatred toward reading, his sense of failure and discouragement will almost surely hamper him no matter how much he tries to improve. Patience and sympathetic understanding are absolutely essential. Occasionally parents become so baffled or fretted by what seems to them to be laziness, or stubbornness, or lack of effort that they do not use good judgment. "Why don't you do as well as your cousin Helen?" "You could read if you'd only try!" are the kinds of reproaches thrown at the helpless child all too often. They only confuse him, worry him, and increase his difficulty.

HE MUST GO AT HIS OWN SPEED

Children should not be expected to live up to the achievement of an older brother or sister, of a twin, or of a friend's or relative's child. Discouragement is sure to mount when unfavorable comparisons are constantly dinned into his ears. It is surprising, though, how hard it is for us grown-ups not to push and nag with the mistaken idea that this kind of treatment will stimulate a child to try harder.

Getting together with the school is the very first step in helping a child who has a reading difficulty. In some places reading clinics, with experts trained in reading difficulties, are available. We are not likely to have more such centers unless we are interested enough to work for them. Parents need to educate each other, as taxpayers, to the realization that such investments are economical in the long run.

WRITING AND ARITHMETIC

There is as much difference between children in the time they are ready for writing as for reading, because each child's muscular adjustment is an individual matter.

Because the movements involved in handwriting require the working together of very small and fine muscles, a great many schools now encourage children to begin with printing, or manuscript writing. In this type of writing each letter is formed separately, with simple, short strokes, which are much easier for young children.

There is much to be said for encouraging children to begin using a typewriter early. Children in the lower grades have been found to have more to say on paper, and to use a larger vocabulary when they can use a typewriter than when they must write by hand. The results, too, even with mistakes, look like more of an accomplishment than handwriting.

By the time a child is in first grade, he is not only interested in numbers, but there are many times when he needs to use them.

Perhaps his room is the third from the door in the second hall; he needs to be able to count to find his seat. Perhaps the teacher asks him to choose three other children to play a game with him.

If in his everyday experience at home he has learned to use numbers he will enjoy this practice, instead of being confused and puzzled. But sometimes parents have paid more attention to teaching children to count than to helping them learn the meaning of numbers. Many a 5- or 6-year-old can glibly count up to 10 without having any idea of the relationships between the words he repeats.

There are a thousand and one ways in which a mother can help her children really understand what numbers mean. She may ask her 4-year-old to bring her two spools of thread, or to get three spoons when he is helping her set the table. When he is playing with blocks he will enjoy following suggestions to make towers of two and four blocks.

We are so casual in our conversation with children that we deprive them of a great deal of information that might come in handy. For example, both wool and butter are known to children from their earliest years, yet less than half of our 5-year-olds probably have any idea as to where they come from. Both in connection with general information and with specific needs (like the requirements for good progress in reading and arithmetic) parents can be very helpful indeed. Letting a child figure out which is a 1-pound and which is a 2-pound box of crackers at the store gives him the beginning of discrimination that may be followed up in numerous ways like dividing an apple in halves or counting out 3 of his weekly 10 pennies to put in his bank.

On the other hand, children can go through their early school years reciting their "tables" without really understanding what they are doing, because only rote memory is involved. Parents can help greatly in making numbers meaningful to children by playing parchesi, dominoes, and simple card games with them.

How to distinguish between "larger" and "smaller," "longer" and "shorter," "lighter" and "heavier" can be learned by playing games that involve guessing weights, distances, sizes. Some 6-year-olds will be able to tell what time it is when the clock hands show the hour, but they will probably be unable to grasp any finer divisions of time.

THE "WHY" OF SOCIAL STUDIES

Parents who went to school before "social studies" were an important part of the school day may be puzzled as to what the term means.

A child's school life should provide experiences that prepare him in every possible way for life after he leaves school. Unless a person understands something of the world in which he lives he can't be expected to act very intelligently in it. And now that we are all so close to and dependent on people all over the world, it is immensely important that we understand *how* we are related.

When most families had their own cow, there were no problems of milk distribution. But nowadays, when a family's milk supply may come from hundreds of miles away, children need to learn how a strike or a blizzard may interfere with their having a glass of milk at each meal. Children who live where wheat is grown must get an understanding of how a drought affects not only them and their neighbors, but children in far-off lands to which we export wheat. The city boy must learn how our natural resources can be conserved—why forests should be protected, how great rivers can be harnessed, or saved from pollution by industrial plants—in order to vote intelligently on laws dealing with these things.

Why is it any better to have "social studies" than to have geography, history, and civics as separate and disconnected subjects? Such a change grew out of the realization that our world has changed. If our children are to understand other human beings' needs, they must know the conditions under which they live, how the way they are governed came about, and how our lives are affected by what happens to other people. It is impossible to split human relations and the problems connected with them up into little separate pieces called "subjects."

If it takes a lot of understanding and skill to gain mastery over the physical world, it takes even more to handle relations between people. What can we do to build friendly relations with people in other countries? How do roads, telephones, and automobiles encourage good neighborliness among ourselves? Why do we have rules for the games we play? When many city people don't have jobs, does that make any difference to farmers?

These are the kinds of questions that social studies try, not always to answer, but to awaken children's minds to.

Children show their interest in the kind of information they get in social studies by the kinds of spontaneous questions they ask. Third- to sixth-grade children want to know things like this:

> How did people get divided up? How were countries formed? How did people learn to use oil? Where does the lead in a pencil come from? Do the people of India dress the same as we do? Why do some people have jobs, others not?

This interest in origins, and causes, this desire to have real explanations, points out how necessary it is for teachers to be well informed in the natural sciences, and in those that deal with the way people live and get along with each other.

The school gives children experience in friendly living together and in taking responsibility in dozens of ways. They learn to think of others' rights when they are taught to keep their voices low and their heels from clattering in the halls. They learn to conserve materials by taking good care of their books, and paint brushes, by saving paper and crayons. They begin to appreciate the meaning and value of family life when they learn how our family way of living grew up in answer to the need of the helpless baby for protection.

Social studies try to bind together all the different kinds of learning that used to be scattered about in hit or miss fashion under many different subject headings. Life is more meaningful when it is studied as a whole.

FIRST STEPS IN SCIENCE

Parents who know something of the load of superstition and ignorance many people carry around with them will be delighted to find their children studying science in grade school. The earlier children begin to get the scientific attitude, the better. The objectives of science and social studies are the same: To help children understand their world, and have some idea about how men go about getting useful knowledge of that world.

A child in the grades can get a "head start" toward more direct and detailed study by having problems to work on (like learning how water evaporates, how frost acts or how a magnet works). He learns by real experiences the need of planning how to go about finding out things. He learns to keep an open mind, how to avoid accepting easy explanations not based on facts. Learning to work with others on a problem, and how to go about getting information from reference books are other valuable contributions of simple science experimentation and observation, planned to suit the children's growing ability to think and reason.

MEANS OF SELF-EXPRESSION

We would all like to see our children learn to express what they have to say clearly, whether in speech or in writing. Until a child can write easily he must depend on the spoken word to get across his ideas. This is why it is important that a child have a chance to talk freely and spontaneously in many situations, before he gets to the point of putting his ideas down on paper.

Children who have not been repressed at home are seldom timid about expressing themselves when they enter school. Of course it takes any child some time to learn how to act as a member of the large group he is a part of when he goes into first grade, but within a few weeks he should feel comfortable enough to tell his group about something that interests him, or take part in discussions.

Much of a child's later ease and naturalness in speaking before a group, or his reticence and fear of doing so, depends upon the skill with which his first teachers encourage him to take part. The informal atmosphere of the early grades seems strange to many parents whose school life was in the stiffer, "reciting" type of classroom. But such an atmosphere is one of the best signs that the teacher is not old-fashioned or dictatorial.

Parents can have a share in helping their children get a good start at self-expression. The richer a child's experiences, the greater his vocabulary and his ability to put his ideas into words. The person who is tongue-tied before a social group is not always the one who has nothing to say. But the child, or even the adult for that matter, who has variety in his life is better prepared to make a contribution to a discussion.

Before children write easily enough to put their ideas on paper, they often express themselves in language that is more fresh and charming than any of the written work they will labor over in school later. Teachers and those parents who have time to take down at children's dictation, stories, rhymes, and accounts of experiences they have, are making it easy for these children to transfer their thoughts to paper later.

Spelling is closely connected with a child's self-expression in writing. One of the reasons why children so often find writing letters or school papers irksome may be because misspelled words are invariably called to their attention.

To encourage children to learn to spell we should make use of their natural activities that call upon them to use words. Children making signs for a circus or a fair they are planning, or printing tickets or placards for a play, will go to a lot of pains to see that they get the words right. Parents should use everyday, natural situations that come up to make children word-conscious in an enjoyable way. Words that sound alike but are spelled differently can be made the basis for games in which the different meanings are brought out.

There seem to be great variations in children's natural ability to spell. It would seem that a child who reads a lot would tend to be a good speller, but such is not the case. Such a child may be too deep in what he's reading to watch the details of words.

Parents who try to help a child learn how to spell should be careful to see that their methods are not too unlike those in use in school. For example, learning to spell according to certain rules, which many grown-ups did, is not practiced today as much as is drill on words that contain pitfalls.

Dramatizing what they read about or experience is one of children's great pleasures, from the time they are very little. To be able to lose himself in the character he is portraying is a wonderful way of freeing a child from self-consciousness. It is a form of expression of deep-lying urges that can be a help to the expansion of a child's personality. It is one that parents can aid and abet by providing stage properties and a variety of clothing to be used as costume material. The old trunk dedicated to cast-off finery, old hats, ribbons, lace curtains, and discarded jewelry will be a gold mine for children who carry on dramatic activities.

MUSICAL EXPERIENCE

When children can or should learn musical skills is a problem dependent on much more than age. Not only must children's physical and mental maturity be considered, but also any special ability in music, and their background of experience. A child whose family is much interested in music, even though he may not possess special talent, has an advantage over one is whose home music is never listened to or played. One who has unusually good muscular control will be prepared to begin to play an instrument earlier than a child whose coordination is not especially good for his age. No matter how great or how small a degree of musical talent a child has, the way he feels about music will influence his learning. If he comes to hate it because of being forced to study too young, to practice too much, or too long at one time, his progress can't be expected to be as satisfactory as that of a child whose whole experience with music has been joyous.

Of real value is the provision in the home of opportunities for hearing good music, and for singing together. Learning to enjoy and appreciate good music, both popular and classical, is just as productive an experience as learning to make music, and it appeals to a far greater number of children.

Even those children who at the start seem to be "monotones" can learn to sing. It is probable that lack of experience accounts for the many such children in the early grades. The earlier children are given some help and practice in following a tune without making them strained and self-conscious, the more enjoyment they will get out of their experience with music at school and at home.

Children like to help make musical instruments. Rattles made with gourds or milk cartons, marimbas, triangles, tambourines, or drums can all be made at home. But such activities promote interest only if they are thoroughly enjoyable.

WHAT INSTRUMENTS SHALL THEY PLAY?

The suitability of different instruments for children, when they begin to have an interest in taking lessons, has been much discussed. Musical prodigies who begin playing the piano or violin at three or four, and by their genius upset all rules of

what to expect, have caused some parents to assume that it makes little difference what instrument a child starts with if only he starts early enough.

A little thought given to the matter makes us realize that what we know about a child's physical development runs counter to this idea. Extremely delicate adjustments must be made by the fingers in playing a violin or a flute. This puts the mastery, or even the use of such instruments out of the question with all but a very few children until a high degree of motor coordination has developed. Add to this the extremely sensitive ear necessary to the detection of mistakes in pitch, and it becomes easy to see why the piano is often regarded as the most rewarding instrument for younger children.

Although it is a less "personal" instrument than one they can hold, the piano makes fewer demands on them. Selected children, with special talents, may make very good progress on reed or string instruments. But the piano with its definite arrangement of keys, and its much fewer demands as far as muscular adjustments go, conforms to the child's motor and mental development better than most other instruments.

So much depends on a child's inclination toward music, and the way he is taught, that no definite age can be given as the "best" time to begin learning to play an instrument. Very few children will profit much by beginning earlier than the age of 6.

There are children who have a gift for rhythmic activities, without having some of the other abilities required for achievement in music. For them, dancing may prove a delightful form of self-expression.

In providing such opportunities for children we mustn't forget to leave them plenty of time in which to do things of their own choosing. Childhood is pretty much regimented for a good share of the year by five or more hours of school 5 days a week. To fill after-school hours and Saturdays with music, dancing, or dramatic work so that a child has no time he can call his own is to deny him something no "advantage" can make up for.

HOME STUDY PROBLEMS

Although most educators no longer stress home work as much as they used to, `some grade-school children still have assignments to be done outside of school. When this is so, the time and conditions for study should be carefully planned to keep it from being a hateful chore. Preferably home work should be of the voluntary sort, should grow out of the child's interest in getting further information, pictures, or other material to illustrate and expand what is being discussed at school. Home assignments should allow a child to pursue interests that are truly his own and give scope to his originality. One boy may spend thoroughly pleasurable hours on a map; a girl may take great delight in making her notebook expressive of her taste and love of color.

Unfortunately, too often home work is purely routine—so many problems to work, so many spelling words to learn. When this is true, it certainly taxes a parent's cleverness to make home work anything but irksome.

Children need freedom for active, outdoor play after being confined in school for hours. For this reason, the study period should not come right after school. Just before or soon after dinner may be a good time. Most children like to have a little relaxation before going to bed, so to leave some study until the last thing at night is questionable. The conditions surrounding home work should be such that the child isn't interrupted or distracted. A comfortable chair, and a desk or table where the light is good, are essential. Some children like to study in the family group, but the chances are they will settle down to business and get their work over much quicker in a separate room. If they study in the same place every night they will get more done, because they don't have to spend time adjusting to an unfamiliar situation. Only children sometimes do slightly better work at school than those with brothers and sisters. This may be connected with the fact that they can study undisturbed. On the other hand, some adults have very pleasant memories of working with a group of brothers and sisters.

Oftentimes a child will get his home work out of the way more promptly if it is sandwiched in between radio or television programs. This has the advantage of discouraging dawdling; many times a child *thinks* he is studying when he is really aimlessly reading words over and over.

Because of the feeling some older people have that home work is desirable, some of the things educators have found out about it are worth knowing:

1. Children who spend a lot of time on home work often do little or no better than others. A dull but conscientious child may plod away endlessly at home work, but lack the ability to make a better showing at school on that account.

2. Many teachers find that home work doesn't seem to be much of a factor in raising a child's marks at school. This is a good point for parents to keep in mind who are very ambitious for their child's school success.

3. On the positive side, there is some small likelihood that a child who has formed the habit of home study in the grades will do better in high school, where home work seems necessary.

4. There are many times when parents ought to help with home work, and would build up a closer relationship with their children by doing so. The school has a responsibility for letting parents know when and how they can help. Their interest in what their children are doing encourages a favorable attitude toward learning.

Study outside of school by young children is useful, apparently, when it is something freely and naturally entered into because of a child's interest in learning. One who begins to make a collection of railway maps, enthusiastically enlisting his father's help, and talking over with him the reasons for different routes, time of laying rails, and so on, is learning something about our country's history, and also about its resources, trade, contours, and settling by people from other lands. But it is the self-initiated enjoyment that makes this valuable.

The home can contribute by helping a child form the habit of putting his time to good use. This does not mean pushing, prodding, keeping children busy every minute, but rather surrounding them with the possibilities for using leisure time productively, such as books, pictures, materials, and—above all—an atmosphere of enthusiasm and ideas.

In discussing children's activities we always come back to how absolutely necessary it is to know children. Because a great part of a child's life is spent in school, it is necessary for parents to know the school, too. Parents and schools should be partners. Too often parents are silent partners, or if not silent, they voice complaints. Why not be constructive? When parents get back of a plan for hot lunches at school, for including family life courses in the curriculum, things begin to happen in their communities.

9

Everyday problems

Always, in trying to explain puzzling behavior, we must first think of what has gone before. What special circumstances have surrounded this child? What kind of adult personalities has he lived among? What things have happened to him?

Not that we should always hurry to "do something" about conduct that perplexes us. Oftentimes what seems like a tough problem will be ironed out as time passes, and the child becomes more mature. Just as there is a "stage" when temper tantrums are to be expected in little children, so with dozens of other sudden peculiarities of behavior. They blow up like a shower and pass as quickly.

It would be foolhardy, however, to toss off any and all bothersome behavior by saying, "Oh, it's just his age!" or, "He'll outgrow it." But we could sometimes save ourselves headaches by going at such things slowly, instead of immediately whipping up a froth of anxiety.

FLEETING PHASES

There's a stage of hitting and one of turning down vegetables; periods when table manners seem to be slipping back into cave-man-with-a-bone days, instead of getting better. There will be crazes that nearly drive *us crazy.*

We don't know much about the meaning of these side trips children take. But we should learn to recognize the difference between them and behavior that really needs study.

When a 10-year-old is completely heedless of the dirt on his hands, does it mean he's never going to learn to keep clean? Of course not. But how 'to tell the difference between things that matter and those that don't? Will Mary's shyness, that seems to result from her being so tall for her age, last? Or will it disappear as her friends start to grow fast, too? Problems like hand cleanliness will finally take care of themselves, but the tallness and shyness may not so easily be solved. Sometimes, though, the puzzling behavior will be a clue to real trouble. Our groping for an explanation may occasionally hit on a sore spot that needs expert attention. When any behavior appears that is disturbing because it is different from a child's usual ways, we might well ask ourselves, while carefully observing him, "Is this something unimportant and fleeting, that needs no special handling? Or is it the outward expression of some hidden difficulty, the child's reaction to something that is bothering or blocking him?" If watching or studying him in relation to the people or conditions that surround him doesn't provide an explanation, expert help may be needed.

Nearly all parents are shocked when their children bring home "swear-words," or use other vulgar phrases. We lose perspective for a moment because our little innocent's lips have been defiled by vulgarity. We forget that a child who is not daily exposed to such language, whose attention isn't called to it as something pretty exciting—by mouthwashing with soap, or some equally stupid treatment—isn't going to use it permanently. He experiments with it just as he does with anything that's new. Or he may use it in order to "belong" to his "gang." If we don't get excited and make an issue of it the novelty will wear off, and the language will be forgotten.

If we act shocked or show a child that we are disgusted, all that we succeed in doing is to drive him into being very careful not to use the disliked language in our hearing. If we forbid him to play with the child from whom he picked it up we are handling it negatively, instead of trying to be of constructive influence in the other child's life.

THE ROUGH AND RUDE PHASE

One of the more common phases that disturbs parents is the rude, blustery behavior by which small boys begin to assert their independence after they start school. Because they are "picked on" more or less by older boys who have passed through the stage of inexperience, they may try to make up for their young-ness by being bold and tough. Some, being completely frightened and unequal to the situation, are termed "sissies" or "mama's boys." It is much healthier for a boy to meet the problem by an attacking attitude than by being afraid.

But for a mother to see her sweet little boy suddenly transformed into a "toughie" is hard. Having him come roaring into the house, loudly voicing demands, his feet clattering noisily, his appearance that of a street urchin, calls, she feels, for action. Instead of being glad that he's facing up to the demands made upon him, she is likely to be full of reproaches. How much better if she can congratulate herself on his fist fights, realizing that this is a fumbling first step toward proving his courage, and that the boy who listens to the pleas of his parents not to fight may regret it all his life. They can prove it in other ways? May-Se so, but try to tell a boy that and make it stick!

Little girls do not have to establish themselves in quite this way; their strength must lie along other lines. To be favorably looked upon by one's school mates one needs to stand out in some way. A boy whose physical development is good is more likely to be popular than one with a poor physique. Girls may try to get approval by an outstanding accomplishment or getting good marks, or by having pretty clothes. They may go through a phase of seeking friendships with well-thought-of playmates, and of bickering and jealousy tied up with wanting to be "best friends" with girls who are in the accepted groups. Such behavior although of the same motivation is less noticeable and less upsetting than bloody noses or torn shirts.

TEASING AND QUARRELING

Why are teasing and quarreling mentioned so often by mothers as one of their greatest trials? Isn't it probably as much because they are so annoying to us, as because we are so deeply concerned about their effect on the children?

If we looked upon them as a blessing which is denied the only child we might be nearer to appreciating their true value. For what they are, in large measure, is simply a rather crude and noisy attempt at learning how to get along with other people. Brothers and sisters are very convenient agents to practice on.

There are a number of things that seem to touch off this behavior.

Age differences are the basis for a good deal of conflict. Children of 4 and 7 or 8 and 12, have comparatively little in common. Four wants to play with Seven's precious electric train-Twelve can't stand the "silly" jokes Eight is continually springing.

Clear understanding between children about what things are to be shared, and what are strictly private property, is a help. Room enough to turn around in is a priceless advantage, too, if you can find it and afford it. To arrange so that two boys or two girls of very different tastes or ages don't have to share a room may take some clever handling—but it will be worth it. If they must, plan so that they will go to bed at different hours, have separate closet or drawer space for their clothes. Letting children work out between themselves how their space is to be divided gives them the fun of having their "say" in a matter that is of pretty deep concern to them.

Do your children see too much of each other? Some families expect their children to find more companionship in each other than is reasonable. Brothers and sisters get to know each other so well that there may be less novelty and stimulation in their play than when outsiders are brought in. If we think back we may remember better how very important to us our friends were, even at the age of 8 or 10. A family bent on keeping down the annoying bickering and teasing will import children and also encourage their youngsters to go to their friends' homes.

Differences in interests between the sexes naturally result in some clashes. But how important it is for boys and girls to have a chance to learn something about each others' tastes and interests early in life. There are going to be a great many more things they agree about than those they disagree on. Let's hope that continues into their adult relationships. Let's not forget that the ages we're considering include those very years when the two sexes become very stand-offish toward each other. By the age of 9 or 10, boys and girls increasingly shy away from the simple acceptance of each other of early childhood. Perhaps this is nature's way of laying the groundwork for a new appreciation in the teens. Whatever the answer, there is a time when it seems fairly common for boys to turn up their noses at girls and girls at boys. Part of this is only the attempt to establish the importance of one's own sex—for boys and girls in whom natural differences have not been exaggerated by different treatment and training enjoy each other thoroughly, when their interests run in common. But try as we may, we cannot get the average 10-year-old boy to want girls at his birthday party.

It is a good thing brothers and sisters do squabble and pull hair. If they bottled up all jealousy and ill will we might never guess it existed. As it is we get a chance to find out what's causing the rub. When the teasing is one-sided, it leads us to stop and think. Is Ann's picking on her little brother related to the joy with which the relatives greeted the birth of a boy in the family where girls had been in the majority?

Once we have unearthed some clues as to what lies behind undue and unfair teasing, we can take steps to remove the causes. Taking stock of our own behavior will often reveal that we have not been giving enough consideration to the special and different needs of each child. Perhaps we failed to notice that Jane, at 11, is being allowed many more privileges than Lois, now 13, was at the same age. Is it surprising under such circumstances that Lois picks on flaws in Jane?

Have we considered whether Jim's orneriness before supper may not mean he has been overstimulated (the neighborhood boys he plays with are all older than he), and is so tired he is ready to jump on his little sister at every move she makes? Maybe he is the goat so often among the bigger boys that he finds it a great relief to take it out on someone.

No one really knows how much teasing and quarreling should be passed over as normal. But it is probably true that if we could shut our ears to it oftener than we do, and not step in and settle differences, we might find that our children did not suffer. As often as not our efforts to stop the annoyance of loud voices result in our protecting one child unfairly.

SO YOUR CHILDREN ARGUE!

Family life without arguments would be as impersonal as life alone in a hotel. In a family each one's ideas and beliefs and feelings touch everyone else; almost everything anyone does or thinks tangles with the life that is being led in common.

After all, what is so disturbing about having children argue? Could it be that while they are very little, and we parents have the upper hand, we get into the habit of "shushing" them if they disagree with us or have ideas that don't fit in with ours? Shouldn't we be pleased instead of upset over children's tendency, as they develop, to have more and more ideas of their own, and to want to put; across those ideas? It's more comfortable and quiet around the house without arguments, yes. But isn't it true that we tell children to "pipe down" when they are arguing with us or with each other, largely because if they were always docile and obedient it would save us from having to think?

Perhaps we need to distinguish between arguing, which means reasoning, and wrangling. One means trying to clear up or prove the worth of a point of view; the other turns discussions into hot and angry conflict. When this latter is indulged in, it often means that children are rebelling against unfair treatment, are resentful, jealous, or envious.

A parent needs a clear head in order to listen, observe, and be able to decide how much importance to attach to disagreements. But only by doing this can we tell whether "something needs to be done" or whether the picture is one of wholesome growth toward so-called adult ways of settling things.

What do children argue about? Everything under the sun— their interests and concerns are that broad. Why do we get annoyed? Because so many of their discussions seem pointless, or trifling, or take time, and interfere with things we think are more important? Or is it ever because we are too busy or too lazy to think up good answers? We enjoy listening to the hot, rapid-fire arguments of town meeting types of programs on the air. Why do we object to them in our own homes? Instead why not take some tips from such programs?

People who take different points of view on a platform or on the radio have to line up their facts and reasons. Perhaps a family that held to this same standard could do away with some tiresome, useless discussion. It would help children to understand the need of fortifying themselves with facts; of the silliness of holding a point of view that is merely the result of personal feeling, with no solid factual information back of it.

Children nowadays need practice in thinking as perhaps they never have before. Events and difficulties, whether on the other side of the world or on ours, are affecting our daily lives in ways that even children can see. Perhaps this gives us a better chance than parents of an earlier day had to help children get into the habit of considering many sides of a question.

One of the things that comes up in children's arguments (as in adults') is "rights." When Pat argues that he "had a right" to use Bunny's mittens, his own being wet, we have a chance to show how often "rights" must be compromised; how if he had asked Bunny for them it would have saved trouble. When Janet argues that she has a "right" to do what her friends are allowed to do, investigation may show that she actually has some privileges they don't have, or that we have been holding the reins too tight. We want our children to be wary of accepting harmful ideas and prejudices thoughtlessly. Ought we not then to welcome their growing ability to test and weigh *our* suggestions?

DAWDLING, WHINING, SULKING, TATTLING, AND CHEATING

Dawdling is usually a very minor problem, but it's often little things that make us cross, and so lead to friction.

It seems to be in the nature of human beings to poke, fool around, dawdle, delay when bored. That's why dawdling over dressing comes to the fore about the time children start school. The business of getting into clothes has ceased being exciting and novel. It's old stuff, but not old enough to be done speedily and automatically.

Except, that is, when there's a very pleasant prospect ahead. It's worth while, for that reason, to make breakfast as much fun as we can. A child who has a *reason* to get dressed, for example, whose friend is going to call for him, or who has a new turtle to take to school, hustles into his clothes in no time. We may get tired of thinking of ways of making a child look past the dressing, to the interesting *next* thing, but it is worth our time. This stage won't last forever, you know. Removing distractions often helps. Keeping the puppy out of the bedroom and the toys out of sight will keep them from distracting the child. Have Jim dress in another room if Junior keeps making him giggle by deliberately putting his shoes on the wrong feet.

Whining is something else again. It means that somehow you've led your child to believe that this is the way to get attention. You've got to counteract this idea. Give him devoted attention when he *doesn't* whine; be ready to listen to him, not just to say "uh-huh" absent-mindedly; save up little jokes and funny poems to tell him at times when he's around the kitchen, watching you roll out piecrust.

Maybe someone in the family is a whiner? Maybe the child Is copying him. Maybe you're overworked, and need a change. Whining may mean that the child is adopting a self-pitying attitude. Find out *why* the child fancies he's abused or short-changed. Make sure he isn't. Then stop commenting on the whining and forget about it.

Occasionally, whining is the first indication we have that a child is ill. Then, of course, he needs medical attention.

Sulking suggests that a child is bottling up things he should get off his chest. It may mean (1) that he has an undue idea of his own importance; (2)that he's not learning to "take it" when things don't go his way, and he feels baffled to know how to proceed; (3) that he really is misunderstood, that he is not given a chance to explain his feelings.

Commenting on sulky behavior, telling a child to stop sulking, makes him feel even more blocked, and probably will only increase his inability to act and his tendency to withdraw.

It would be interesting to know whether sulkiness is more common in children who have never been allowed to talk back to their parents. A child of 6 whose mother is outraged at his calling her a "dumbbell," instead of taking such an outburst in her stride, may be the one who retreats at 10 into the sulks when faced with almost anything that makes him angry.

If sulking really becomes unresponsiveness and depression, expert help is needed.

Any unhealthy retreat should be a signal for us to provide outlets for the child's emotions. Often, helping a child find an activity with which to busy himself will be the most helpful way of resolving his immediate difficulty. In time, with a better understanding on our part of how to avoid provoking such a crisis, he will work out ways of handling his emotions more acceptably.

Tattling is unpleasant, but so common in young children as to seem more normal than otherwise. What does it mean? It suggests, of course, that the tattler is weak, and has to come to an adult for support. Common sense tells us that all children are weak on occasion; but when a child is constantly pointing out the unfairness or bad conduct of others we may begin to suspect that he is in need of a different kind of help from that he asks. He needs to be built up, to feel equal to situations. Then he won't need to be on the lookout to pull some one else down.

Tattling that lasts after a child is old enough to understand the ugly meaning of tale-bearing betrays insecurity. The job his parents face is not how to make him stop tattling, but how to make him feel secure. One child will need more praise for his efforts to be fair and square; another, more responsibility; a third may need help in laughing off minor injustices, in developing more of a sense of humor.

Cheating (as was mentioned on p. 33) is another indication of inability to "make the grade" in the personal struggle **for** satisfaction. Whether at games, in school work, in getting out of tasks or by doing them poorly, not playing fair tells us something about the fears of the child and the standards he is setting up for himself. If his belief in himself is not sturdy we must try to find ways of building up his morale.

Is he living and playing in a group that is so highly competitive that he feels he *must* come out on top, even by unfair means? Has he been overindulged at home, so that he is unused to struggle? Are his longings for achievement out of keeping with his ability, so that he has become one of the "I-won't-play-if-I-can't-win" kind of child?

Once parents understand the possible meanings of such behavior they can usually supply children with the help that makes them feel equal to situations.

HOW IMPORTANT ARE GOOD MANNERS?

A good deal of unhappiness comes to children because their parents have pretty set ideas about manners and children have none. (Well, hardly any!) They have natural friendliness and cheerfulness, though, that go a long way to make up for their failure to see why "Hi!" isn't always as acceptable a greeting as "How do you do?"

Some children are made into little puppets with a thin layer of social varnish. Usually such manners do not stand up under hard wear. Unless the courtesy that we try to make habitual in children is real we are not doing them much of a favor. They may have a whole bag of tricks like how to hold their fork right and how to take off their hat to a lady, and still be rude and selfish. It is more important to teach a boy not to push ahead of someone at a counter in order to be served than to be sure he remembers to get off a bus ahead of the girl he's with, in order to help her down.

Real politeness comes from the way a person feels. If we help children to have kindly feelings toward others their manners in expressing their feelings will pretty much take care of themselves. One of the good ways of letting children in on the secret of good manners is to be considerate of them.

This is the basis of all good social conduct. Manners are catching. There is contagion in pleasant morning greetings by parents; in the "excuse me" that springs to our lips when we have been thoughtless of our children's rights; in the "thank you" that a child learns from the gracious consideration with which kindness is received, in quiet voices, as much as in shrill ones; in warm friendliness for those who do us services.

WHEN IS TEACHING NECESSARY?

There are all kinds of little special ways of feeling at ease in social situations that a child will not have practice in at home. How to behave in a restaurant or on a train; how to thank one's hostess graciously at a party—all these have to be taught. The child who learns many of the "proper" things to do is going to be a more comfortable adolescent when he begins to have wider social experiences.

There are many good books on manners written for boys and girls; and while boys under 12 will be inclined to scoff at such fol-de-rol, they may take a peek at the books that interest their sisters. Leave them where they're conspicuous.

Many mothers cleverly arrange for their children to help them when they have guests. Awkwardness and embarrassment disappear when a child has something to do, like showing guests where to put their coats, or helping to pass sandwiches.

Discussing why certain ways of doing things have come about helps children to recognize the need for many of our social customs. Just as the buttons on a man's coat sleeve, that were useful when his lace ruffle had to be kept out of his plate, now serve no purpose, so some of our social customs are useless relics. But most of our polite ways came into use for a reason, and if they make our relations with others easier and smoother, they're worth holding on to. By talking about these things we can help children discriminate between things that are simply superficial, and those that show good breeding because they are more than skin deep. Men used to take off their hats when women got into elevators; nowadays they realize it is much more considerate to leave their hats on than it is to jab people with their elbows while trying to take them off.

Parents can help their children to converse easily. "Small talk" is of very little consequence in one sense, but immensely important when it helps others to feel comfortable. The family that fosters discussion of current events, that listens to the children's opinions about movies, television or radio programs, is at the same time making it possible for them to express themselves in a group.

Teen-age children who are beginning to take part in social life a good deal often complain that they "don't know what to talk about," especially among strangers or members of the opposite sex. Those who have, from the time they were quite young, been welcomed when they took part in adult conversations will have had enough practice by the time they reach the so-called awkward age so that it needn't be awkward. The 10-or 12-year-old will be glad to have mother provide a few phrases that can be used when greeting people, or saying "good-by" at a party.

To hear their parents' guests discussing interesting questions is an important part of children's education. They can be taught not to demand more than their share of attention just as they are taught how to shake hands cordially. Children should have learned well before the age of 6 not to interrupt, and not to "show off" when there is company.

Children must have real interest in other people if they are to find it easy to talk with them. The family that is warmly friendly, that has many kinds of visitors, makes its children aware of other people and their feelings. Being a good listener is as important as knowing how to talk; so children who recognize how much people like to talk about their own interests are readier for social experience.

There is more value in commenting often on a child's good responses than on what he forgets or does poorly. If we don't call attention to blunders we will avoid making him self-conscious.

NERVOUS HABITS

"Nervousness" is a sort of rag-bag term. We put this label on any kind of behavior that puzzles or bothers us. A child who bites his nails is called "nervous"; so is one who wets the bed, is an overactive chatterer, or a restless sleeper. We often assume that such behavior suggests a highly sensitive, easily agitated child. In some cases unstable emotions may be in part due to the original nervous equipment with which a child was born; but we must not forget that his surroundings have had a lot to do with the ways he responds. We neglect to ask ourselves if *we* are responsible for our children's being nervous. Perhaps our habits (a screechy voice; whining about how much work we have to do; darting restlessly from one thing to another) are enough to force nervousness upon them. It is easy to expect a child to conform to more mature behavior than he is capable of. A child who lives with excitable adults is not helped in developing serenity and calmness. *Some* sort of pressure is, or has been in the past, back of stuttering, masturbating, making grimaces with the mouth, bed-wetting, or any other habits that are hard to understand. Nervous habits involving the mouth are the most common of the various ways of expressing pent-up energy.

To center attention on the nervous habit itself is to confuse, almost paralyze, the child. Our business is first to get at the underlying causes. The form the nervousness takes is only a symptom.

ENURESIS (BED-WETTING)

If a child of school age still wets his bed, here are some of the things to look for. Was learning to keep dry over-emphasized from the beginning? Did he ever really learn to keep dry? If the wetting is of fairly recent appearance, what events in his life may be tied up with it? Did something occur that was a threat to him, for example, bringing home bad marks, giving up having a room or bed to himself, or being punished for sex play with other children? Is jealousy of a younger child making him fall back into babyish ways—ways that certainly gain him attention?

If he has wet the bed off and on for a long time, look for some chronic condition that weighs on him, and that he is helpless to do anything about. Do his parents distress him by continual bickering? Are they divorced or separated, so that he's batted back and forth between them, hearing one criticize the other? Is he the dull one in a bright family, so that there's a nagging ache of self-distrust where his self-confidence ought to be? Is he under a strain because he has just entered school?

Most important of all, has he been made to feel miserably ashamed of his habit? Punished, scolded, told he could help it if only he would try?

Once a child becomes fearful of not being able to stay dry, and is pestered by efforts to make him do so, his anxiety piles up. He's afraid outsiders will know of his trouble. Instead of being a help to him—which he can usually count on—his father and mother blame him.

What we can do for a child who has this trouble is to try to take whatever load he's carrying off his shoulders. He should not be punished, or scolded, or made to feel disgraced. All the effort should be in the direction of making him comfortable and light-hearted and capable. We will do more by building up his strength and self-belief than by any amount of criticism.

If he is emotionally excitable, things that overstimulate him must be avoided. He, more than the next child, needs consistent handling—not to be allowed all kinds of favors one day, and then jerked up short the next. He needs to have solid ground under him, to know where he stands with his parents. He needs occupations and interests that will encourage concentration, instead of restless running from one thing to another. He will probably need to be shielded from harrowing movies, radio dramas, and tragic news items more than the average child. His sleep and rest requirements must be kept constantly in mind.

He will welcome practical ways in which he may learn to overcome his habit; like having an alarm clock in his room that will awaken him in the night (bed-wetters are usually very deep sleepers), or a room alone, so that he will not be humiliated by having others know about his lapses. He needs to have his mother and father feel, and show, confidence that he will get over his difficulty all right. He needs to know that they are accepting him, not frowning on him as a nuisance.

If, when everything possible has been done to rid a child of any worries (like his school progress, his relations with other children, or money difficulties at home), he still persists in wetting his bed, professional help should be sought. If there is no child-guidance clinic in the immediate vicinity, local or State departments of health, welfare, or education are always glad to give information as to where the help of a child psychologist or psychiatrist may be found. Rarely indeed is there a physical cause back of prolonged bed-wetting, but this possibility should, of course, be ruled upon by a physician. Circumcision is never a cure.

Sometimes enuresis, like other nervous habits, begins when the child is under some sort of strain, and remains, though the

strain has been relieved. When a parent comes to the conclusion that the bed-wetting is just a "relic" that fact in itself
may help to clear the atmosphere.

In many cases, a change of parents' attitudes, and their encouragement will make it no longer necessary for the child to
return to the helplessness of babyhood.

NAIL BITING

Nail biting is another sign of strain. To attack it by applying a
bitter-tasting substance to the fingers is almost never of any use,
because it does not do away with the tension that is causing the
habit. Forever calling a child's attention to it does more harm than
good; it only gives him something more to feel tense about.

The most constructive way of helping to overcome this habit is
to free him from any known causes of fatigue, overexcitement, or
worry, and to look patiently for causes that do not appear on the
surface. Children have been observed to be especially prone
to bite their nails when they are inactive, and at the same time are
being emotionally stimulated. Sitting for a couple of hours at a
movie, reading a thrilling story, or working on a tough arithmetic
problem are examples of this kind of pressure. Having plenty of
whole-body activity and much freedom for letting off steam cuts
down the need for nail biting.

To help a nail biter by letting him have gum to chew or an
apple to eat when he is studying is to recognize the need of
giving him a substitute for the undesirable activity. But most of
all, removing causes of worry or anxiety must be relied on to
rid children of this, or any other nervous habit.

10

Fears, worries, frustrations, and their outlets

As children learn more about the world we might expect them to fear only those unpleasant or harmful things that it makes sense to be afraid of. Actually, this is not so. Instead of worrying about such realistic things as being run over, they turn out to be afraid of being attacked by tigers or gorillas, or of finding a lion under the bed. Fears of the dark, of "spooks" and unearthly creatures, of robbers and criminals, are so common as to make it obvious that children have picked up these dire imaginary dangers from stories, movies, or television; from over-hearing grown-up discussions of unpleasant things; from other children; or from lurid newspaper accounts of crime.

A fear of storms, very prevalent at 8 or 9, is an exception, storms being something most children have experienced. It is often learned from adults who have never outgrown their own childish fear of thunder and lightning

114

Just as young children fear things they cannot understand, and are unprepared to deal with, so older children, in being afraid of the weird and mysterious, reveal that it is things that are unfamiliar and unexplained that worry them. When children have bad dreams, things they fear appear in them, such as frightening animals, criminals, and robbers. It is highly important, then, for adults to guard their conversation, and not discuss things before children that may, because of their ignoreance, cause them to worry.

Fewer farm children are afraid of dogs than city children. This points to how much familiarity with an animal has to do with dispelling fear. The more information a child has about any situation that may cause him to fear, the more familiar he is with ways of dealing with such situations, the less likely he is to be fear-ridden. There are great individual differences in the number and degree of children's fears. If a fear persists, and parents' efforts to deal with it fail, expert help and careful investigation of the causes may be necessary.

Some thoughtless or malicious adults purposely frighten children, so it is essential for parents to know the persons with whom they leave their children. While it may seem less important in middle childhood in comparison with the impressions children may get in the pre-school years, the very fact that the school-age child is more conversational, and has broader interests, makes such chance contacts important.

Movie, radio and television thrillers contribute to children's fears, even though they usually are not the underlying cause of these fears. Children who already feel disturbed and uneasy are more apt to be impressed deeply with what they see and hear in these ways. It would be fine if parents could see every movie their children went to, beforehand, but this is a practice limited to a very few homes. It is possible, however, to use lists of suitable movies printed in magazines for parents. When it comes to radio and television we can sit in on children's programs. If we think a certain program undesirable we can plan our children's activities so as to have other interesting things to compete with it. A sensitive, highly imaginative child will naturally have to be protected more than one who takes things casually; and sometimes it will be less harmful to let a child listen to a program that all his friends talk about than to give him a feeling of being thwarted and "different."

Just as a child is less emotionally upset by an exciting movie if his father or mother is with him, so a child probably feels more secure if an adult listens with him to the radio drama, and talks over the story with him afterward. By discussing a movie or radio play with a child we can point out absurdities, that heroes are not killed off, that things will come out all right in the end; thus helping him to have a little perspective.

Part of the enjoyment of such things comes from being "safely" frightened. There is a tingle and thrill in taking part (even at second hand) in adventures, if one feels secure. The fun of coasting, of climbing to a high place, or of diving comes in part from the knowledge that there is an element of danger, but that things are under control.

FEARS CONNECTED WITH THE SELF

More subtle than these fears that children recognize and talk about are fears connected with the child's self. All of us know what it is to feel adequate or inadequate, the result of having played our part well or poorly, as the case may be. A child is in the midst of creating the part he is to play. His expectations of himself, the things he achieves, must not fall too far below his belief in his own ability. If Billy has created for himself a role of being able to do all the things he sees other boys of his age doing he must succeed at them or fall back on daydreams. If in the daydreams he is strong and quick, can bat or catch a ball efficiently, he doesn't for the time being have to admit his disappointment in his own lack of skill.

The vaguer fears that children have of not being liked by other children, of not getting good grades in school, of not being as good looking as others, are made up of two things primarily; first, of failures to live up to their own ideal selves; and second, of not being able to play the role their parents have dreamed up for them. If Billy's father has set his heart on his son's playing baseball as well as he himself did, then Billy has a double job on his hands. He has to avoid lowering his self-esteem on two counts—his own and his father's estimate of him.

Thus each child has to defend himself from attack, both from without and from within. It is a ticklish business to keep destructive fears from undermining the self-confidence of the child, a confidence so necessary to mental health.

Boys, in particular, are expected to "become someone," because our society has long placed on them the task of money making and providing for the family. They are bombarded with questions as to what they are going to "be" when they grow up; while little girls less often have this question put to them. (Something is expected of girls, too; they are expected to get married; and by the teen age some girls are fearful that maybe they won't have a chance!)

Perhaps the great stress placed upon boys in this matter of "making good" in the world has something to do with there being more stutterers among boys, of boys being greater "problems" in general, so that many more of them turn up in child-guidance clinics, and also become delinquent. Although they are expected to take an aggressive stand toward life, when they do they are frowned upon!

That our tradition of the man as the breadwinner is affecting children is shown by the worries boys as young as 10 or 11 have about getting a job when they leave school, especially those whose families have economic worries.

WORRIES HAVE MANY ROOTS

By nature, some children are much more serious than others. Those who are dependable about bringing things from home are the very ones who have their shoulders bowed under their teacher's reminders. The others are lightheartedly heedless.

No one knows how much responsibility we can expect of children at various ages. We need research on this. But common sense tells us that children should be protected from worry.

A tendency toward worrying unnecessarily may start in early childhood, when the 2-year-old has to be separated from his mother for months, and from then on feels, deep down where he doesn't know it, that the bottom may drop out of his life again.

Sometimes children worry because their parents are worriers: they've heard father express his concern about losing his job or mother harp on her poor health.

Children must learn to laugh at hard luck and mishaps if they are to face things with courage. Parents' practices have a lot to do with whether their children habitually cross bridges before they come to them.

One of the basic kinds of fear that has to be considered as a possibility is that of being unable to accept the independence that children normally look forward to. Children are eager to be bigger, to have more privileges and wider experiences. Jean looks forward impatiently to going- to school; Jack is sure he could manage a bicycle, like the older boy next door. How often their conversation has to do with being "grown-up"!

But occasionally a child is afraid to grow up. He prefers to remain at the baby stage. When this fear (rarely, of course, expressed or realized) is present it may point to his parents' unwillingness to give him a suitable amount of independence, which eventually results in his sinking back unhappily into a state of effortless dependence.

Dick, finding that the other boys laugh at the precautions his parents take about his health, and the fences they put up around his activities, quotes as an excuse the "heart murmur* a doctor once mentioned. He is afraid to face a future in which he must many times meet with ridicule or criticism. Or Mary, sensing that her mother is unhappy and overworked, unconsciously dreads growing up and possibly having the same kind of marriage.

These fears, because they go unrecognized, are much more harmful than fears of concrete things. Unlike a fear of dogs, or fires, they will not be outgrown with experience, but only strengthened.

Timidity, shyness, a tendency to worry can't be brushed off by being talked about. Unserviceable personality traits need opposite traits built up to work against them. Perhaps Don, who is physically small, and not particularly attractive, does extraordinarily well at soap carving. This ability may serve as a basis for developing self-confidence, and lead to the discovery of other skills that will help him to hold his head high among the other fellows. Julie, whose shyness makes her terror-stricken at the idea of going to a party, will feel less self-conscious if her mother arranges beforehand to have just two or three girls over, informally, letting them get their own lunch, color Easter eggs, or learn to knit. There will be few awkward conversational gaps if they are busy doing something.

If every child had some accomplishment (not in the sense of a parlor trick) that set him apart just a little, be it clarinet playing, baking cakes, acting, identifying birds, raising calves or fine tomatoes, the results would be almost immeasurable in the way of offsetting weaknesses.

WHICH AGE DO WE LIVE IN?

The witch doctor or medicine man tries to scare away sickness; the scientist, frustrated by lack of knowledge about a disease, searches instead for a remedy or a way to prevent it.

Children, in just the same way as the witch doctor, try to scare away things that baffle them by what we call "compensatory" behavior. A child who has a hard test coming up pleads illness. One who is frightened at facing the consequences of having damaged his friend's bicycle tries to put the blame on the child who caused the spill. A girl who feels awkward and ill at ease may try to cover this up by talking and laughing too loud. All such ways of acting point to the need of helping children find real ways of getting out of jams; of helping them get away from the witch doctor, and closer to the way the scientist goes at his problem.

It is common for us to look at the symptom, or the child's action, and forget that there is something behind it that demands search for what can be done in the way of prevention or remedy.

PRACTICES AND SITUATIONS THAT MAKE ESCAPE NECESSARY

/. When we deny children the chance to develop

The answer to this, of course, is to let children lead their own lives. We get so much practice in looking after children while they are little that it becomes second nature! We continue to say, "Have you got your mittens?" when it would be better to let Harry learn to remember for himself by having cold hands.

Because it is hard for a parent who has few or no other outlets for affection than through his children to "let go," a widowed or divorced mother often has to watch herself in order not to become too closely tied up with her children. An instance of the often unconscious attempt of such mothers to hang onto their children is having a child sleep with them even up into the teens.

Conflict between parents can bring about an equally bad emotional tangle, for one of them is fairly likely to turn to the children for comfort, or to champion the children as a way of venting resentment against the other parent. For parents to be happy with each other is one of the best ways of making sure that children feel secure and self-confident. There is an atmosphere about such a home that encourages a forward-looking attitude toward life.

Some parents make things too easy for their children. What happens when a 10-year-old makes excuses at school for not having work ready when it was supposed to be? He's not going to find his teacher as tolerant as his indulgent father, who lets him get by over and over again.

Sometimes an attitude of dependence continues beyond its natural limits because parents do too much for their children. A child who never has to make any personal effort to get what he wants knows little about the joy of achievement.

2. When we encourage children to excuse their mistakes

Finding false excuses for poor behavior or mistakes that we are criticized for is known as "rationalization." We think we are using our minds, when in reality it is our emotions that are dictating our explanations. This is not a real way of meeting difficulties, but it is so commonly practiced by everyone that often it goes by unnoticed. We try to explain our failure to be on time instead of admitting the truth—that we didn't get up early enough.

Unwillingness to take blame is a human trait, rather than a childish one. But a marked tendency to shift or escape blame by making up reasons for behavior betrays, whether in an adult or a child, a lack of belief in oneself. Our shoulders should be broad as we grow up to carry the weight of our mistakes and omissions.

If we find a child excusing himself by falling back on reasons that don't hold water we must suspect that we have either been too hard or too easy on him. Whichever turns out on close scrutiny to be the case, the child's efforts to make his conduct seem reasonable warn us to change our methods.

Perhaps we pin children down too much. When we say, "Why did you spend your whole quarter for candy?" and Edgar replies, "Well, I had to treat the other boys," knowing full well that he ate most of it himself, we practically force him into getting out of being blamed. He knows we don't want him to spend the money that way.

Being too easy on a child can cause him to try to slide out from under, too. Carol loses her rubbers, forgets at whose house she left her sweater, and lets it go at that if we lavishly provide clothes without teaching her to take care of them.

Often, too, we ourselves set an example of rationalization for children to copy. We need to watch our step.

3. When real-life pressures force children into daydreaming

Everyone daydreams. Reality is too harsh, or too dull, to live with every minute. But when a person retreats from life to such an extent that he enjoys the dream world more than the real one something is wrong.

The school-age child is usually too busy enjoying other children and exploring the things there are to do, make, and see to spend much time daydreaming. But when a child finds his school work too hard, or so easy he gets it done in no time, when he's either bothered or bored—daydreaming comes easy. His imagination supplies a more satisfying place to be.

Such daydreaming can be taken care of by supplying more challenging work, or by making the work easier, whichever is necessary. But when daydreams mean escape from intense un-happiness, the answer isn't simple.

Being unpopular, having a disturbed home life, feeling unequal to things are some of the common causes of a child's drifting off to build aircastles. Each case has to be handled differently, because no two children have exactly the same set of reasons for being dissatisfied with life. We can't provide a palace for Jean, who dreams about living in a mansion because she can't bear to have her friends see her family's shabby living quarters. But we can do *something* on this score to make her feel better. We may be able to see that she gets into a club whose meetings are held at church or school instead of in the members' homes.

4. When we deny children the respect they are due as people

Those inferiority feelings we all have twinges of now and then probably get their start in childhood, when unless care is taken we get the impression of being too little, too unimportant to count. Instead of being tolerant of children's ideas, we should respect them. When children are disregarded, or made to walk on and off the stage like unimportant extras, it's no wonder they sometimes become retiring and standoffish.

Children get laughed at a good deal, and it hurts. When they innocently say things that show how naive and ignorant they are, the amusement adults show makes them curl up inside. They'll get taken down enough by their schoolmates if they're too uppity; they don't need to have us pile our superiority on so thick.

FEELING "UNLIKED" OR UNWANTED

Real or imaginary differences from other children are some-times responsible for feelings of inferiority. When a child has a deformity, it is easy to see why he may shrink from contacts, unless great pains are taken to build up his self-confidence. But 6ometimes it is only in a child's imagination that something is wrong with his appearance. Maybe he's heard his parents say he's the "image" of an uncle he dislikes. Or, a little girl may hanker after black hair and eyes and hate her blondness. Such fancied causes for withdrawal into one's shell can be done away with only by persons with real insight. A parent's show of pride in the child's assets, assets that he may be unaware of, will help a lot.

Ridicule by playmates often causes distress when actually the teasing may be the result of envy. This sometimes happens if connection with clothing, when a child despite his protests, per-haps, is better dressed than others. A visit to the schoolroom often helps a mother to be a better judge of what to buy for her child. If other children are wearing corduroys or plaid lumber jackets, her preference may need to be overruled in order that her child may look like one of the crowd.

Sometimes withdrawing or escape behavior is caused by a feeling of being unwanted, unloved, or misunderstood. Children who come in the middle of a family sometimes fail to get as much attention as the oldest and youngest. Parents are conscious of the needs and demands of the oldest because they are facing such demands for the first time. It is an old story when the second or third child starts to go to school, to learn to read, to go to parties; there's no longer so much excitement and freshness about these events, for parents. The youngest child always remains in a sort of special place, too. It's up to us to make sure we don't neglect "middle" children, indignantly as we would deny this possibility if we were taxed with it.

WHEN SCHOOL IS TOO HARD

School experience, too, can have a part in developing feelings of inadequacy. Not to "know the answer" happens to children over and over again. How can the piling up of failures and mistakes, with the emphasis that's put on marks, and the acclaim that goes to those on the honor roll, keep from affecting children's belief in themselves?

We can do a lot to prevent loss of self-esteem by avoiding comparisons—comparisons of children within a family, or among schoolmates. Emphasizing a child's own efforts in school, rather than his standing in the group, and measuring him according to what may fairly be expected of him should be our aim. This involves, of course, a knowledge of his general mental level, which the school is always glad to discuss with parents.

MASTURBATION

It might seem more appropriate to take up masturbation in connection with sex education than with inferiority feelings. But it is purposely placed here to bring out strongly how often this behavior becomes associated with fear and guilt, and hence with feelings of inferiority.

Practically all children at some time or other handle their genitals. The handling of the penis or vulva in young children is as natural as touching any other part of the body. Because touching these sensitive areas gives pleasurable reactions it is easy to see why stimulation of them is frequent. The fact that the boy's penis is so much more prominent than the girl's vulva may make play of this sort more natural among boys than among girls, and may account for the apparently greater frequency of masturbation in boys. From birth on, a boy's attention is called to his penis by occasional erections.

Literally, masturbation means causing sex excitement by manipulation of the genitals. But in children of the ages we are talking about it gives a wrong impression to use the word; for a very large proportion of what we call masturbation is probably not that at all, in the actual meaning of the word. Some children undoubtedly do stimulate themselves to excitement in this way purposely, but much of what disturbs parents is of no more consequence than any other of the ways in which children respond to minor restraints or enforced inactivity. It is necessary, too, to make a distinction between handling of the genitals as a chance, playful pastime and their handling as a compulsive nervous habit.

Punishment is the last way of checking such an activity, whether it is merely a casual one or a deliberate attempt at providing pleasure. Scolding a child, or in any other way condemning the behavior or showing disapproval, only brings guilty feelings. To make a child feel that he is "bad" may do lasting damage to his personality. If the activity is the result of emotional strain or deprivation, we must go beneath the symptom, and get rid of the cause. The less tension and worry there is within the child the less reason there is for continuing the habit.

Since this kind of act carries so much more social disapproval than one like biting the nails, a child's parents find it hard to deal with masturbation wisely. If they understand that severity and blame may only drive it underground they may find it easier to keep from showing a reproachful attitude. As children grow older and sense more keenly what things are not acceptable they also become more skillful at hiding behavior that is frowned on. To encourage a child to practice self-stimulation in secret is far from what we want to do; but it may be exactly what we do if we make him feel guilty.

Part of our strong feeling may be the result of the old notion, so long in dying out, that masturbation leads to insanity. There is certainly nothing to justify such a view. So far as we know, the only way in which masturbation can be even remotely connected with mental illness is the possibility that feelings of guilt over a socially disapproved act might add to a person's emotional confusion.

A child who is happy and feels wanted, loved, and unafraid has little to escape from.

When a child feels emotionally secure, and is given the insight and understanding appropriate to his age, a serious problem is not likely to develop. The parents of a child whose handling of his genitals becomes a persistent habit need to examine very carefully what circumstances in their child's life may be causing the underlying emotional problem. If they find themselves unable to understand what is causing the child's difficulty, they may want to seek such help as that provided by the highly skilled workers in a child guidance clinic.

OVER-AGGRESSIVENESS

So far we have described children who are retreating from trouble, who are only pretending to meet it. Sometimes children go at their problems more combatively. But taking a blind swing at an enemy without knowing where he is doesn't make much sense.

Children need to have aggressiveness in their make-up, aggressiveness in the good sense. But there is another kind of aggression—acts that annoy, bother, embarrass, or make trouble for other people. Sometimes only a few people are concerned (as when a 7-year-old is rude to his parents) sometimes more (as when a 10-year-old steals at school). Such behavior is useless as far as solving the child's smoldering problem goes; but it has a nuisance value. it calls our attention to the fact that he is in trouble, and so sometimes we do something about it. Too often we do the wrong thing, but at least we are made so uncomfortable that we see there is a problem.

Lying, stealing, bullying, destroying property do not seem like very healthy ways to act, but at least they force parents and teachers to recognize that something is wrong.

LYING

No one is 100 percent truthful even though we all disapprove of lying. We associate lying with all sorts of other bad behavior, because it is so often used to cover up. Because we connect truthfulness with honesty and sincerity, qualities that we want to encourage, we sometimes bear down heavily on a child's failure to live up to our vague ideals.

If we would remember that lying is usually a child's attempt to protect himself we might try to make it less necessary for him to resort to lies. If Tom falsifies in order to escape punishment, isn't our method of punishment questionable?

Fear has no place between parent and child, and yet a great deal of children's evasion of the truth is based on fear. Harsh or severe punishment can be responsible for a lot of such trouble. The more Tom fears what his father will "do to him" for borrowing a friend's bicycle or going to a movie that his parents have forbidden, the more effort he's going to make to keep his father unaware, even if he has to lie about it.

Children can't be forced into truthfulness. Rather, we should try to help them feel that the consequences of telling the truth, even under hard circumstances, are more satisfying than the other way round.

When we push a child into a corner by our insistence we run the risk of making him feel that we distrust him. Few things can more quickly undermine his feeling of security. If we act horrified when we "catch" a child in a lie, what can he do but be more careful next time not to get caught?

Many parents feel it is their duty to force a child into admitting he has lied, when simply saying they are sorry if he feels there is something he can't tell them about might open the way for free discussion later. If parents are uncertain as to whether a child is telling the truth it is better to assume that he is, and trust to later events to make things clear. Kindness and belief and readiness to help are much more likely to break down the barrier of a child's fear than is suspicion or accusation.

"There is no better, more logical, nor surer way of developing the habit of truth in a child than by permitting him to live in an environment where he may have truth as an example to imitate."

This is just as true now as when Dr. Douglas Thorn wrote it for the Children's Bureau years ago. It means that scrupulous honesty about paying a child's carfare, after he's 6, will influence him to take for granted that he must pay the increased amount necessary to get him into a movie after he's 12. It means, instead of boasting about "getting by" with the undercharge of a shopkeeper, calling attention to under, as well as overcharges. It means facing the music when the traffic policeman whistles us to a stop, instead of trying to pretend we were not at fault It means being honest in all matters, instead of resorting to trickiness, or methods that come just within the law.

When a child's lies do not seem to be based on fear but are, rather, exaggerations or stories made up out of whole cloth we'd do well to ask ourselves whether they reveal something important about his underlying desires. By the time a child is

7 o r 8 h e should be able to distinguish between the real and the imaginary. Suppose 8-year-old Hilda's teacher expresses interest in the trip Hilda has told her we are going to take— a completely nonexistent trip. Embarrassing? Yes! But our concern should be with why Hilda needs to build herself up in this way, rather than with stopping her from making up such myths. Does she feel her family isn't important enough? Is her life so tame she craves excitement, and knows this story will call attention to her? Something is back of it. The "lie" is only an aggressive but wasted attempt to set something in her life right. Often, though, we may be wise to meet the "tall story" by calling it a "good story," and realizing that the child is practicing her newly discovered imagination.

STEALING

Stealing is cut off the same piece of cloth as lying. We abhor the idea, and are so shocked if a child steals that here again we may make a wrong move.

One of the puzzling things about stealing is that so often children take things they have no use for. Again it is an impulsive, wild effort to work out a disturbing inner conflict. Maud was a 9-year-old who had recently lost her father. Her mother was forced to go to work and to leave Maud in the care of the woman who ran the boarding house where they went to live. To her mother's astonishment and chagrin Maud began to take things (but always things she had no use for) from other people's rooms. This pointless stealing was her frantic response to so sudden and complete a loss of all that had made her feel secure.

Punishment in this case would be like pushing a drowning person under water. Such an instance shows why no general rules for handling stealing can be laid down; each individual child's behavior must be considered as a symptom. A physician doesn't treat symptoms. He uses them as clues to guide him in finding out what the disease is.

Stealing is one of the most difficult of all behavior symptoms. It may not be too farfetched to suggest that perhaps children, sensing the seriousness with which grown-ups look on it, sometimes steal just because this is one of the surest ways of expressing their resistance, of reacting against inner turmoil. This is not, of course, a conscious motive, but a blind, molelike, underground one.

Edwin is a boy who is frightened and disturbed because he is not wanted by either his father or his mother. They have been divorced, and each has remarried. After a few months with one some excuse is always found to send him to the other parent. In his distress he takes to stealing, though he has plenty of pocket money. Punishment hasn't the least effect. Without knowing it he has chosen a way of letting out his bursting emotions that is intensely bothersome to his parents. They would not be so concerned if he got sick, or moped, or even ran away. But this behavior humiliates them because it is socially disapproved. In such a case it is easy to see why the conditions causing the child pain must be done away with before his stealing will stop.

By stealing money with which to buy treats for other children youngsters sometimes let us know that they are craving more popularity and friendship. Stealing sometimes gives a clue to important desires of a child that are going unfulfilled: when 10-year-old Tom pleads for a ball his mother should find out how important the ball is to him before she says she can't afford it.

What good does it do to label behavior? No good, of course, unless it helps us to get back to the causes, and do something about them. To describe Sue's crying spells, when she locks herself into her room, or Bill's refusal to pay any attention to requests to come home on time, is the first step in searching out the causes and trying to do away with them.

Whether a child is actively doing things that worry us, or is *not* doing the things we would think natural, our main concern should be with finding out the why's.

WHEN STEALING IS NOT STEALING

The 6-year-old who takes pennies from his mother's purse may or may not be "stealing" depending on his previous training. Usually, he is only doing something he has seen his mother do. Having as yet very little notion as to the meaning of money, except as something you hand over in order to get something else, he may take it to use just as he would the hammer or the scissors. He does not have to ask to take these; no more, at first, does he ask when he takes money.

Because money is regarded in a very different light from other useful articles, we must begin guidance very early to keep children from making such mistakes. We have only ourselves to blame if we run into problems because of our failure to teach the difference between using the hammer, which you put back, and the pennies, which you don't.

"Run and get a dime from my purse" is a common way of dealing with a child's request for money to buy something he needs or wants. If it is as simple as that, why should he bother to ask next time? Parents are not always scrupulous, either, in their dealings with children. "Borrowing" from a child's bank, without his permission, to pay the paper boy, is as much a breach of faith as it is for him to take nickels out of his mother's purse.

The problem of having children take money may never arise, but we make it very tempting for them to do so when we are careless about leaving money lying around or when we do not know how much small change there is in our purse. Being re- miss about such seemingly little things leaves the way open for a habit to start. Begun in all innocence, it may continue after a child knows better.

"But I want to be able to trust my children," you say. But you don't trust them to handle your best dishes, while their movements are still jerky and impulsive. Perhaps their minds are no more ready to use judgment about taking money than their muscles are prepared to carry a pile of plates safely.

Things to a child are either "right" or "wrong" as his parents tell him. His resistance to doing acts labeled "wrong" is built up only gradually. While a child is gaining strength, we should do all we can to help him, not put temptation in his way.

One of the good arguments for giving children an allowance early is that in this way they begin to appreciate the difference between what is theirs and what is not. We have all seen 3-year-olds struggling with and only dimly grasping why they must let mother's books alone. Constant and careful training should result in a pretty clear understanding on the part of a 7- or 8-year-old of how untouchable the property of others is—whether the property is the next door neighbor's flowers, the apples in the grocery store, or the nickels on the newsstand.

RUNNING AWAY

Since running away from home or school is actively doing something about his trouble, it is aggressive behavior that makes us sit up and take notice, even though it is also an "escape." There are almost as many reasons for running away as there are runaways. Children run away because they feel unwanted at home or unloved, because school is so utterly boring or hard or confining. They run away to try to escape from themselves, when they are conscious of not living up to what is expected of them, but are unable to do anything about it. During the depression of the 1930's many ran away because they felt they were a burden to their poverty-stricken families.

When any of these reasons has been dug out, remedies can be found. Harder to solve are those cases in which the need for excitement and a life that offers more opportunity for self-expression are the motives. We keep lengthening the time in which a child is dependent on his family, and increasing the age at which a boy or girl is allowed to leave school to go to work. Along with this has come a reduction in the ways in which youngsters can earn money or feel that they are useful community members. These things make it necessary to think ahead toward the adolescent stage in which breaking away is a vital part of growing up.

Overnight hikes, bicycle jaunts of several days, camping, taking part in Cub Scouting, having workshops and tools are some of the ways of satisfying the hankering for the freer life that our earlier pioneering took care of. The sprouting adolescent urges in girls are not always the same as those of boys, but they exist. To look "grown-up," to have more opportunities for independence are important to both boys and girls. To ignore the expanding needs of the school-age child, instead of being sympathetic and understanding, is to court trouble in the teens. Fewer girls than boys run away, of course, but they may "run away" from us psychologically or emotionally if we allow a gap to appear between their needs and our efforts to meet them half way.

Some special family concerns

1. THE ADOPTED CHILD

To take a child when he is a baby means that parents have a freer hand in his care and guidance, and the child does not have the insecurity that often comes from having had to adjust to a number of different homes. The younger a child is when he is adopted, the more years of sheer pleasure his parents have as they watch him develop.

But parents who adopt an infant or a very young child have a special obligation for the very reason that he does not remember any other home. That is, to make him familiar with the fact of his adoption as he grows, and so protect him from the shock or injury of learning it later from somewhere outside.

Why tell him at all? Because experience has shown that not doing so, instead of being a kindness, can lead to tragic results. Over and over again parents who have tried to keep from their child the fact that he was not their own have had the sharp sting of having the child learn it suddenly or even cruelly from outsiders. It is impossible to be sure that this won't happen if he is not informed of his adoption by his parents.

Such an experience is totally unnecessary. A child who gradually becomes aware of his special place in the family adjusts to it bit by bit, in keeping with his increased understanding of its meaning. At 6, he is aware only of the superficial differences between being an own and an adopted child. He is content with a very simple explanation, provided his parents give it in a casual way, without becoming emotional.

A child who knows that he was a "chosen" baby, picked to fill an empty place, has a warm sense of being wanted in a very special way.

Adoptive parents stand in special need of reassurance. They sometimes feel that their friends and neighbors are looking at their child with critical eyes, and judging them accordingly. Actually, adoptive parents themselves are the ones who are most critical of their methods and the "results." Uncertain as to just what they may expect of their child, they sometimes watch him more closely than they would one born to them. Of course the behavior and abilities of an own child would be just as unpredictable, but it is hard for them to realize this.

It is not only useless, but dangerous, to worry about the material with which we work when we bring up an adopted child. Our job is to be sure that the influences with which we surround that child will bring out all the best that is in him. An adopted child will bring out a lot in his parents, too, that they didn't know was there. As he takes hold of his parents' emotions, he plays an important role in shaping their attitudes. They grow as much as the child they adopt does.

The tragedies that sometimes result when children are placed in homes that are either above or below their general mental ability can be avoided by very careful study, both of children and prospective homes, before placement. The importance of going to adoption agencies of high repute is obvious.

At the same time, adoptive parents, like any others, need to watch themselves to see that they are not too ambitious, or ambitious along wrong lines, for their children. The fear that many people who adopt children have that they will not "turn out right" sometimes leads to pressures and overanxiety that actually help to create problems. Adoptive parents should value highly, and strive to achieve, the relaxed fear-free attitudes that help to insure happy family life.

2. STEPPARENTS, "IN-LAWS," AND GRANDPARENTS

Stepparents

What kind of problems do stepparents have that own parents don't? For one thing, they often have to compete with a memory about which a child has strong feelings. Even though he may not actually remember his own father or mother, he may have had the absent parent built up to heroic proportions, if no longer living, or heard him spoken of with contempt or hatred if there has been a divorce.

A stepmother, being more closely associated with the children, has to adapt in more ways, probably, than a stepfather. Too, she takes the place of the children's first and most intimate love object. A woman is lucky if she takes on stepmotherhood while children are very young. In this case they have neither formed such long-time attachments for their own mother, nor have they—in case of her early removal—been under the care of a number of different people, as is often the case with older children.

The first thing a newcomer in a home needs to do is to prepare herself for liking the children. This doesn't mean that she should immediately begin to be demonstrative with them, or expect them to call her mother, for love is a matter of slow growth. Until a stepmother can really *care* about them, she must make up her mind to accept them. If she thinks of the children as "spoiled" or "naughty" or sees many disagreeable things about them she will probably have trouble. But if she thinks of them as victims of unfortunate circumstances, who look to her to make their situation happier, unpleasant behavior will not seem so bad.

If a child's own mother needs to understand what children are like, and how they differ from one another, such understanding is even more vital to a person coming in without knowledge of all that has gone before. Jack's smarty, pert manner, Jill's utter indifference to the looks of her room, the habit both children have of trying to dodge tasks and errands would be baffling to anyone. But how much more baffling they are to the new mother who has no idea how to arouse their interest and cooperation. This means she must take things very slowly. To rush in and expect the children to fall in love with her as their father has would be a bad move. In fact, their father's interest in her may be an extra hurdle. They may resent her at first because she takes away some of his attention.

Such a ticklish situation demands a period of watchful waiting. It means developing great insensitivity to things that would hurt her if she let them.

One stepmother made a very clever move by immediately arranging for her 12-year-old stepdaughter to have a permanent wave, showing her sensitiveness to the little girl's despair over straight hair. Another sided with the boy (after discussing the matter privately with her husband) in his pleas that he was old enough to have a bicycle.

Own children place ability to cook high on the list of "important" things about a mother. Surely taking a little extra trouble to find out what children's favorite dishes are isn't too obvious an approach to lifting oneself in their esteem. Being helpful about a child's school work, sensitive to his hurts, and jubilant over his joys are short cuts to understanding.

Turning a blind eye to a child's shortcomings is something even own mothers could afford to do oftener. New mothers will find a useful technique with a child who has a chip on his shoulder is not to see the chip!

The new parent may need to bring about some changes of habits. Children may have poor eating habits, or a generally haphazard way of living. The new mother is almost bound to want to introduce her own ideas into the family living pattern. We can't expect change overnight. We often defeat our own ends by being impatient, by not realizing that it takes a long time, even under the best conditions, to substitute new ways for old ingrained habits. If Bobby has "gotten by" for years without eating cereal, or without hanging up his pajamas, we may have to go the long way 'round in getting him to change. (We may have to become acquainted with the radio or television characters who eat cereal to such good effect!)

As with own parents, things will have an enormously greater chance of going smoothly if the mother and father agree on the general guidance of the child. Seeing eye to eye on every issue is too much to expect; but if both parents have the same approach, and realize that they will need to meet on a common ground of compromise many times, they will be able to work things out.

"In-laws"

Why do we so often take it for granted that one's in-laws are hard to get along with? All of us have seen examples of the greatest understanding and enjoyment between individuals whose ties were made by marriage only; but we are apt to remember the unhappy examples the same way the one marriage which breaks up strikes us more than the five or six marriages that do not.

We often forget that there is a basis for mother-in-law jokes, going down into the roots of our behavior. It helps, sometimes, to recognize the origins of conflict.

It was mentioned in the discussion of a child's affection (p.46) that the first person a baby usually loves is his mother. While deep, strong attachment to one's mother (and father) seems to be related to the ability to make a happy marriage, too strong an attachment may lead to unhappiness. A boy who thinks his mother is just about perfect, and who expects to find the same traits in his wife that he admired in his mother may hurt his wife. He compares her with his mother or tends to follow his mother's advice too slavishly. The shoe is on the other foot when a girl has admired her father so much that she expects her husband to measure up to him.

The results, to either partner, are sometimes irksome. The more we understand such harkings-back to our parents, the more we will be able to throw them off, realizing that they should long ago have been outgrown.

Not only will family relations be happier and more relaxed if we can look at these remnants of our childhood loyalty and dependence with some humor, but we will avoid creating made-to-order sources of antagonism for our children to contend with when they are married.

Grandparents

Grandparents are often a source of inspiration to children, in addition to being the best-loved of all their family connections.

The presence of several generations in a household works out successfully only in proportion to the good emotional balance of those concerned. If any one member of the group is unstable and demanding, he or she can make it so unpleasant for the rest that they may be forced into appeasement. As with other dictators, the more an individual is given in to, the greater becomes the pressure of his demands.

Children are often the victims when the ideas of two generations clash. The mother who is exasperated at the way *her* mother interferes with the handling of her children, sometimes snaps at the children rather than at the older person.

When differences can't be harmoniously settled, parents have to decide whether the risk to the child's mental health is great enough to warrant hurting the older person's feelings. As children become mentally mature enough to appreciate some of the problems involved (which will vary greatly with different children) they can be taken into their parents' confidence. They are likely to be very fond of their grandparents, despite his or her peculiarities, and they will be in a position to learn some good lessons in politeness, self-control, and gentleness. Younger children need to be protected from the confusion resulting when methods switch with the person who is in control at the moment.

When extreme old age makes it very hard for a person to be flexible, and unhappiness over no longer being useful results, everyone concerned will be better off if arrangements can be made for separate living. Too often the oddities of senility, creeping up by degrees, create a situation that is very hard on children, as well as on adults.

On the other hand, having grandparents to visit, whose whole-souled and unselfish love gives children a backlog of faith and
respect, can be a great asset. Nowadays, grandparents are so familiar with the new knowledge about raising children that they very often are helpful in aiding and abetting parents' methods or guidance.

3. CHILDREN OF DIVORCED PARENTS

Even though parents may try to persuade themselves that divorce is not going to harm their children, they are shutting their eyes to the truth. To the best knowledge of some of our most experienced mental health specialists, divorce is always harmful to children. It may be more harmful., or less harmful, they say, but it always harms them. It hurts the parents, too. They are bound to grieve and be unhappy over not being able to provide the normal home life they expected to share with their children.

Parents who have after careful consideration come to the conclusion that a broken home will be less damaging than the conditions resulting from their trying to live together are bent on finding ways of making children suffer as little as possible. What are some of the ways in which they can protect their children?

The parent who has custody over the children can try to see that the life lived by the children is as stable as possible. While we cannot say that security is any more necessary at one time than another in a child's life, the young child, who cannot grasp the reasons for sudden, upsetting changes, is in especial need of protection. He depends to a greater extent upon the physical security of the same walls, the same familiar faces and the same voices than the child who can express his questions and feelings, and to some degree understand what is told him.

Children need two parents. A father and mother each have something special to contribute, and there is no substitute for a home that has them both in it. But it has to be assumed when parents have decided upon separation that what each supplies the children involved may be more desirably given as an individual. The pulling and hauling that goes on while they are living together may be more disastrous than the broken home.

That children are more usually given over to the custody of the mother is in large part the result of the mother's traditional role as homemaker. The law is slow to recognize changing situations in our culture, one of which is the frequency with which mothers now spend as much time away from home, either at work or at play, as fathers do. In such instances, the care given by a mother may be no better either in quality or quantity than the care given by the father. With the increased understanding of the importance of the father-child relationship, the question may be asked as to whether a mother is any more important to a child than a father.

Because most of us are easily fooled into believing what we want to believe about ourselves, divorced parents should watch their attitudes toward the other parent. A woman may think she is being very careful not to infect her children with her feeling about her former husband and yet, in subtle ways, poison their minds against him. "No, you can't have a new coat this year. Your father hasn't sent enough money for me to buy you any decent clothes!" is the kind of insinuating remark that puts the blame on the father, though he may really be quite blameless.

The man who feels bitter toward his wife may unthinkingly show the children, when they are in his care, that he doesn't care a rap about their mother's ideas or practices. Or he may actually, and vindictively, encourage their acting counter to what he knows would be her wishes. Either parent, or both, may in their disillusionment, impart feelings of pessimism and gloom, and may, without being aware, set up distrust of the opposite sex.

While the relief that comes to a man and woman through divorce may be great, failure to have made a success of a venture of which great things were expected is often such a painful experience as to make many parents turn to their children for solace. This overdependence on the children may not be very wholesome for either the children or the adults.

Why family break-downs occur

The very fact of divorce suggests that at least one parent, and possibly both, were unable to make the personality adjustments necessary to successful marriage. Young people need to understand more about the ingredients that must go into marriage to make it turn out right, such as the possession of common interests, attitudes, friendships, and associations, with emotional balance to leaven the whole relationship.

Knowledge of the personality factors that seem to be associated with happiness in marriage may help parents to try to surround their children with influences that encourage such qualities.

Some things turn up over and over again in the background of people who are happily married. They are lack of conflict with parents, and strong attachment to both mother and father; early discipline that was firm but not harsh, with mild and infrequent punishment; and parents' frankness about matters of sex. When these background factors, pointing to a happy childhood, are present in a child's life, they apparently strengthen his or her chances of being able to create a successful marriage partnership.

So far experiments in studying marriage are in the nature of feelers put out with the idea that any information we can gather about the sources of happy marriage relations is all to the good. Family life is such an intimate and private affair that it will take very delicate measuring devices indeed to get to the heart of it.

4. CHILDREN WHO HAVE SPECIAL HANDICAPS

Children who are handicapped mentally

Mental retardation is associated with slow development. Sometimes such slowness is so obvious that a child's parents realize, by the time he is 6, that he cannot profit from going to school.

But there are many children who, although not mentally defective to that extent, are slower in learning than the great majority of children. This group of children, on the borderline of feeble-mindedness, need special understanding and care quite as much as, if not more than, the more severely handicapped. With proper guidance and education, they can become useful and happy members of society. Left to fail year after year, to fall farther and farther behind their classmates, they may become hopelessly maladjusted, a weight on their parents and on society.

It is always a blow to parents to discover that they have a child who is slower than the average. The knowledge often comes to them with such a shock that they cannot at once accept it. Of course they should not accept such a pronouncement unless it is made after careful study by a psychologist, thoroughly capable of judging the child's ability. But to refuse to admit the truth when it is pointed out as the result of such observation and testing may do the child a great disfavor. It means prolonging the time when he must struggle to live up to expectations that are too high and endangering his happiness through failure to give him good early training.

The sooner parents know the degree of their child's retardation, the better they can plan for him. To subject him to the experience of entering first grade along with children whose mental age is 6 years, while his may be only 4, is to risk his becoming discouraged, befuddled, and laughed at. Only when such a child is placed in the hands of a very understanding teacher indeed can he be at once protected from the unthinking remarks of other children who call him "dumb," and given work that he can do successfully.

Such a child, entering school perhaps a year later than is usual, may reflect the excellent training he has had at home. If his mother has patiently taught him the necessary things, like learning to dress and care for himself, has let him have the pleasure and satisfaction of "helping" her in the thousand and one little ways that are at once educational and enjoyable, he will be ready to be cooperative and helpful at school.

If it is important to give normal children praise for hard-won achievements, how much more important it is to encourage the slow child when he has made some little advance. Things that seem so small they are hardly worth noticing may represent real effort: learning to set the table, to sort the dried beans, to take a hard tumble laughingly are all worthy of loving comment.

The very fact that a child's intelligence is limited makes it all the more important that his emotional development be given special attention. (This is important, too, for the reason that there are still people who think of mentally handicapped children as not having very strong emotions.) Because he cannot judge so well which things are worth while to be afraid of or angry about, the emotional habits he forms—habits his parents are largely helping him to develop—must serve him to an evan greater extent than in the case of normal children.

If a child's mental handicap is so severe that he cannot be expected to make his own way in the world, parents face the question as to whether they should place him in a school where he will get the protective care he needs. Parents sometimes refuse to face the fact that they may not always be on hand to give this care. They occasionally forget, too, that it may actually be *their* comfort and happiness rather than the child's that is being added to by his remaining at home. Will he not, in a great many cases, be better off among those who are not unlike himself in interests and abilities? His presence in the home may not interfere with a normal family life for his brothers and sisters. But is it fair to him to keep him where he will be subjected to a good deal of strain and pain, as he sees them engaging in things he can never accomplish?

Children who are physically handicapped

Among the diseases that still have to be reckoned with as thieves of children's rights are those that keep them from being normally lively and active. Restricting children's activity can have as crippling an effect on their personalities as disease has on their bodies. We must take special pains to try to put ourselves in such children's places.

Physical handicaps may or may not hold a child back, depending on what we make of them. A child with big ears that stick out may actually be as troubled by them as a child who limps is by his limp. The child with big ears may have been twitted about them until he imagines everyone notices them; the other may have had his defect minimized, and his good features dwelt upon. Parents can make even the wearing of glasses a bugbear, and they can make a deformed leg unimportant. "In all times there have been lame kings, crippled field marshals, blind ministers of state; always history has added to their fame because they mastered a physical handicap. Unter-rified, they took as their own the words of Goethe: 'It is the spirit that fashions the body to itself.'"

The spirit of the parent has a lot to do with this fashioning, too. If a child who has had rheumatic fever is made to feel that he is permanently "different" from other children; if his weeks of rest in bed, and the cutting down of his activity for a long time afterward make him expect coddling, the effects of this treatment can be almost as damaging as the disease.

It is a nice question as to how to give such a child proper protection, and at the same time prevent his outlook from becoming crippled. The same situation exists whether the child's handicap results from polio, or cerebral palsy, or any other disease, blemish, or deformity.

In the case of diseases like epilepsy or cerebral palsy, for example, it is not only the child's parents who must be aware of the need of a positive and optimistic approach, but neighbors, friends, teachers, and relatives, too. All need to remember that these children are *just like other children,* aside from their handicap. Emphasis on their likeness, rather than their un-likeness, helps them to take a constructive attitude toward the handicap.

Pursuits and hobbies

WHY AND WHAT CHILDREN READ

"... if you will note down the names of the child classics, you will see that Germans, English, Americans, Russians, Danes, Swedes, Italian, and French are all the most friendly of neighbors ... you will not find a single country that does not admire, even sometimes more than its own best books, books that come from the four quarters of the globe. The world of childhood is tolerant ..."

"Smilingly the pleasant books of childhood cross all the frontiers."[1]

Whether or not we have given any thought to reading as a means of increasing world neighborliness, we all want it to be a source of leisure-time enjoyment and profit to our children.

We parents sometimes appear to fall into two groups: those who lament, "My child's nose is always stuck in a book!" and those who worry because their children never read.

[1] Paul Hazard, *Books, Children and Men,* Boston. Horn Book, 1944. p. 141.

We are most concerned with the great middle group who lie in between; those who may, or may not, depending somewhat on our guidance, turn into readers—readers, that is, of much beyond the comics in the newspapers, the captions under the welter of photographs in the picture magazines and the capsule-condensed but unrelated jumble and hodgepodge of information that overflows the racks of every newsstand. As one writer puts it, people "think a newsreel in the movies gives them the news. They think their minds are working when they are full of unrelated pictures, pictures, pictures, and compressed pellets of articles."

Not until they are about 8 or 10 do children begin to have much choice about what they read. Until then they must depend upon what their parents and teachers supply. But by this time, they are beginning to read simple full-length books and are able to use their school or neighborhood libraries. At least those fortunate ones who have them do. At about 9, too, boys' and girls' tastes in reading begin to take separate paths, as their interest show increasing differences.

Girls read more books than boys do. This is probably only a reflection of boys' greater interest in active play. However, boys read more magazines than girls do. In addition to detective story magazines, they read magazines dealing with science and mechanics, a hint for parents to provide such magazines if they want to encourage their sons to busy themselves with distinctly creative activities.

The fact that "series" books are first in popularity with both boys and girls does not mean that they are as good as their high favoritism would indicate. It only means that they are cheap, easy to read, and easy to get hold of because so many children have them. Children like them, just as they like the comics, because the same characters appear again and again; and because, whatever they may lack in the way of literary style, the story is always lively. Because one of our main objects during the early school years is to make reading enjoyable the series books serve a useful, if limited and temporary, purpose. Instead of denying children such sugar-coated series books we had better see that they are also well supplied with books of unquestioned literary value. Then their reading diet will not lack style and beauty and really worth-while content. Children who have access to well-chosen books of good quality will not, after they are able to read easily, spend any great amount of time on books that haven't real worth.

WHAT ABOUT THE COMICS?

The commonest of all free-time activities of 9-, 10-, and 11-year-olds is reading the comics, either in newspapers or books. The average child at this time keeps up with 23 comic strips regularly. They are as much a part of his daily life as his meals.

What accounts for this tremendous popularity, and what effect does it have?

Children lead much more restricted lives than they would like to. They would like more adventure, more variety than their humdrum everyday family and neighborhood life affords. The comics provide this. In them the most outlandish things happen, and the child, identifying himself with the swash-buckling hero, can break loose from all the restraints of actual life. Just as adults read adventure and mystery stories to "escape," so youngsters escape into the hair-raising world of the funnies.

Perhaps if we let children come to grips with life, if we did not constantly hinder them in their efforts to learn how to do hard things, and if we offered them more opportunities for desirable excitement and adventure, they would rely less for pleasure on escaping into imaginary perils and hazards.

Comic books have their good points. Whenever a child reads one he is exposed to many words, sometimes hundreds, that are new to him. Study has shown that the bulk of the words used in the comics are standard English, not slang. In reading difficulty they are usually about fifth- or sixth-grade level. The younger child may be really improving his reading ability when he reads them, but he could equally well be adding to his vocabulary by reading that heightened his imaginative powers and gave him a feeling for the magic of words and ideas.

The harm the crude drawing in comic books may do to children's dawning sensitivity to beauty may seem of importance to only a few, but the possible influence of the violence, vice, and crime which children see pictured in comic books is another matter. Some of our ablest psychiatrists are alarmed at the reflection of comic-book learning which they claim to see *in* the children they study.

Even setting aside the hardening effect of daily exposure to cruelty and vulgarity, there remains the more subtle influence of seeing fun poked at certain races or nationalities as inferior; or of having certain people looked down upon because they perform "menial" jobs. When comic strips picture family life in coarse and stereotyped ways—mother-in-law jokes, plate throwing, and the like—they are certainly a negative influence.

If the comics need improving, who more than parents should be concerned? When they group themselves for action, parents can be pretty effective in exerting pressure, and have on occasion brought about desirable changes even in comic strips. Their main effort, however, should be in the direction of supplying counter attractions powerful enough to lessen children's dependence on second-hand experience. Children who have real-life outlets for their craving for adventure, who can expend their energy in satisfying personal accomplishments, will have only a tiny fraction of time left over for the comics. By the age of 12, such children's interests will have broadened to such an extent that books of adventure, books about "how to make" and "how to do" will be eagerly sought.

Many millions of comic books are sold each month as evidence that they feed some hunger in children, or serve as an outlet for pent-up aggression. What there is about our society that makes necessary dependence on such forms of entertainment is anybody's guess. One guess might be that parents are too busy or too far off from the world of childhood to give thought to the prevention of frustrations in their children.

TO BE A DOER IS IMPORTANT, TOO

Important as reading is, it is always a secondary experience, a substitute for the real thing, or at least a preliminary to it. Most adults would rather travel than read travel books. On the same basis it might be argued that the child who doesn't read much is better off, if he is having actual experiences—making things, playing with animals, making discoveries about nature, going places where he can see for himself—than if he is falling back on vicarious experience through books.

Of course the time comes when a child must read if he is to get further enjoyment and profit from real experience. Even the simplest chemistry experiments require reading; boys and girls who are going camping want to read about how other campers have handled their problems.

We are all more or less curious as to how famous people "get that way," and have been impressed with a statement that appears over and over again in their life stories that in childhood they "read everything they could get their hands on." This ravenous appetite for books doesn't account, of course, for their "greatness." But it does remind us that much precious time in a child's reading years may be lost if we do not provide easy access to good reading material. At a time when many good reprints of outstanding books may be bought for as little as a quarter or a half dollar, and when traveling State or county libraries increasingly make available even to families remote from cities the best of children's literature, we have little excuse for not acquainting children with the infinite resources in books.

Nor should we forget how important it is that children's reading be given some direction. This, in the light of what boys and girls actually read, may be more necessary in the case of girls than of boys.

From the days when, at 9 or 10, girls first become interested in stories of home and school life and boys in adventure, there is a possibility that without guidance they may be exposed to such a narrow range of interests as to cripple their intellectual development. As they grow up those who, from childhood on, have tasted little else but a one-sided diet may limit their reading to the superficial "success" or detective fiction in our magazines, or "best seller" love stories.

Parents, without being highbrow, can do a lot to change this picture. By reading aloud, by family discussions, by letting children sit in on conversations with interesting guests, by spending at least half as much on books as on movies, some parents stimulate the interest of their children, both boys and girls, in such a way that those children become effective, lively "stirrers-up" of their generation.

HOBBIES AND SPECIAL PURSUITS

Both boys and girls are interested in collecting things. Sometimes these are amusingly trivial, like match folders, streetcar transfers, playing cards, or campaign posters. The aim here may

be simply to be able to brag to other children with similar hoards; the greatest value sometimes, the glory a child gets out of it!

But sometimes collecting becomes an educational experience. A child begins to gather post cards from different places; or, his attention first caught by a bright-colored beetle, begins to observe more closely other insects whose names he must look up. Then, presently, we have a young naturalist on our hands. To be indifferent to ways of furthering a child's interest is to lose a point of contact with him, and possibly to cut him off from an exhilarating achievement.

Working with tools has come to be a favorite occupation for many by the age of 10. Obviously, if boys and girls have had no opportunity to handle tools until this age, they are not going to be as skillful as those who began to use hammer and saw and vise and plane when 4 or 5. Taking pictures, producing plays, making and playing musical instruments, working with electricity—all these and many more are favorite activities of children, especially of bright children.

Often parents think of certain hobbies—picture-taking or playing musical instruments, for example—as too expensive to encourage. As a matter of fact, the enthusiast in almost any field finds his hobby an asset to more learning involving serious effort on his part. A boy who learns to play a musical instrument may put himself through high school or college by this one skill. The girl who has made a hobby of studying birds or flowers may find herself in demand as a camp counselor. A girl who learns to type for fun may wind up earning pin money by typing other students' papers.

Of course it would be foolish for parents to put money into something which is so untried that they have no inkling as to the strength of a child's interest or ability. Families have been known to sink a lot of money in dancing lessons, only to realize later that their daughter will never be anything but a mediocre dancer. But if a child's ardor and efforts are both marked and lasting he may be willing to sacrifice other things in order to have the equipment or lessons that help him.

A special value of hobbies lies in their giving a child something to feel proud about and to be respected for. If a child is just average in school work he has a special need for the lift that comes from doing something well. Parents, and teachers, too, need to be on the lookout for ways to build up children who do not have much to feel "important" about. Making a collection of costume dolls, becoming expert at drawing maps, gaining an unusual amount of information about some one subject are examples of the kind of specialty that should be encouraged as contributing to a child's mental health.

RADIO AND TELEVISION

Anything that cuts as big a slice out of a child's time as television is bound to have more than a passing influence on him. Whether he watches only 1 hour a day or 3 as many children do, he is being introduced to ideas, customs, words, and events in a bewildering array. Some of what he listens to may be a waste of time or even harmful; but we can be fairly sure that he is also having his vocabulary and general knowledge broadened.

One of the results of television watching that needs investigation is the effect upon children of the extravagant claims of advertisers. When children are bombarded with glowing statements about one product after another, some more intelligent children, at least, develop a somewhat skeptical attitude toward them. Many others less thoughtful get an immense amount of misinformation as well as being influenced in favor of certain products, or developing a habit of being easily taken in by large promises.

The amount of debate and discussion on the air, even though the number of children who listen to such programs may not be great, makes it plain to children that there are different sides to every question. The fact that boys listen to political discussions and lectures more than girls emphasizes again their greater leaning toward acquiring factual information.

One of the drawbacks about watching television is that it keeps children from active, outdoor play. Parents need to think about this seriously. If children have many opportunities for the satisfaction of their adventurous and creative impulses they will not be so dependent on adventure that is manufactured for them. A group of children making a scooter in the back yard will be likely to forget all about going in to watch favorite programs 4 days out of 5.

Parents, even those in large cities where children's freedom is much hedged about, could do more than they do about providing chances for active participation. Sometimes a determined group of parents can get their board of education to furnish a competent playground leader and adequate apparatus for many sports.

One of television's good points is that it brings the family together in the home. But very often, too, conflicts come up because some members dislike programs enjoyed by others. Here is an opportunity to practice real democratic living by taking turns, compromising, working out ways of meeting needs, according to age and interests, especially when there is only one *set*

The ever-present problem of listening to the radio while studying is a bothersome one in many families. Music furnishes a pleasant background for work, but conversation draws the attention away from it. It has been shown many times that absolute quiet and solitude do not necessarily produce the best atmosphere for work: we concentrate a little better sometimes when we have to make a slight effort to shut out interference. It is better not to make final decisions about whether or not a child can have the radio on while he is studying without being sure it really is a handicap.

Some children's emotions are unfavorably affected by listening to wildly exciting radio dramatizations. Often they dream and have nightmares after hearing them. One of the first things to consider in dealing with such problems is the, radio listening habits of the child. Older children as they gain experience are less affected. Younger children can be diverted from listening to unsuitable programs by well-planned reading aloud, or entertaining games. There are plenty of fine stories and games that interest children of different ages, as well as the parents whose participation makes up a large part of the fun. One of the frequent cries of "middle-aged" school children is., "We wish our fathers and mothers would play more games with us!"

Naturally, most fathers and mothers are not free to play games at the time, just before supper, when many of the children's programs are on the air. But by using a little ingenuity, a compromise may be worked out. Many a child would be willing to forego even a very exciting radio program if he had his father's and mother's promise to join him in a game after the evening meal.

13

Children and money

We would probably all agree that children need to learn how to use money. But how they can best be taught to do so is another matter. We know very little about how people learn to manage money wisely. Most of us learn through our actual experience, if we learn at all!

We say "Experience is a good teacher." But do we put her to work teaching early enough? We take children's "education" very seriously, but do they really learn much at school about how to manage money? And yet when they are adults they will be expected to know how to use money as a tool in spending, saving, earning, giving, and borrowing. It is as if we never let them use a pen or pencil while they were growing up, and then all of a sudden expected them to know how to write legibly.

WHAT MONEY EXPERIENCES CAM PARENTS PROVIDE?

1. Making and following a plan for giving a child money will bring better results than hit-or-miss hand-outs. An allowance that grows as the child's needs grow is one device. Beginning with the very small amounts a 6- or 7-year-old child needs, it can be increased with the child's growing ability to make independent decisions. By the middle teens many children under such an arrangement are buying many of their own clothes. Needless to say, such practice keeps a child down to earth, and gives him a real understanding of the need for sensible planning.

Too often parents give an allowance and then dictate how a child shall spend it. Actually, such dictation defeats their purpose. If a child is told he must save 3 cents out of every dime, or that he can spend only 5 cents a week on candy, he has no chance to use his own judgment. If we (direct every bit of his spending, it remains *our* money, in which case there's little point in calling it his allowance.

Talking over with him questions that come up is another matter. We can point out that if he saves a little of each week's dime or quarter he can buy something he really wants at the end of the month. We can remind him that when he's invited to other children's parties, he'll want to be able to give them birthday presents. Our children nowadays are so well aware of the plight of children in other parts of the world that giving out of one's funds has become very much a part of their thinking. When it involves self-denial it will have more meaning than when it's just a matter of handing on the money they asked their father for.

"BUT THEY WON'T SPEND WISELY"

Of course they won't! They'll throw their money away o» flimsy toys at first, buy too much candy, be "broke" long before the end of the week. Children learn by trial and error, and the errors help, as well as the successes. If Ruthie shortsightedly spends her allowance, forgetting the movie she especially wants to see on Saturday, she'll actually learn something, either by not being able to go, or by feeling the pinch when she pays back what her mother lends to her.

Some parents would disapprove of a loan under such circumstances. It is something for each family to decide. But why not let an 8- or 9-year-old begin to learn something about borrowing? Ruthie's experience now may help her understand what's involved in the mortgage she and her husband may have to put on the first house they buy!

Taking the consequences of rashness is one way children learn. It may be hard for Jack's father not to *give* him the money to repair the window, broken because he didn't listen to a request to play ball farther from the house. But facing an obligation may be a lesson Jack needs very much.

2. A child should never be punished by having his allowance taken away. By doing this we make the mistake of seeming to pay him for good behavior.

Money should not be tied up with discipline in any way, unless through entirely natural consequences, as when Jack has to pay for the window he broke. But in this case it is the *event* that disciplines the child, not his parents.

It is a great temptation sometimes, when a child spends money foolishly, to attempt to control his spending by cutting off his allowance. To do so simply puts off the learning that will have to come sooner or later through mistakes. It may seem that his mistakes aren't teaching him anything; but here, as with other learning, we'll be disappointed if we expect results too quickly.

3. The allowance should be planned with a child's expanding needs in mind. A little experimenting may have to go on at first, and of course additions will have to be made as children take on more responsibilities. An 8- or 9-year-old can be expected to think ahead enough to figure out how often he will need a haircut (though he'll need reminding about saving up the money for it); and an 11-year-old can take on the responsibility for carfare and lunches. It's not so much what an allowance covers that matters as it is that the child should be having a greater chance each year to exercise judgment and foresight

Some of our children's friends will have more spending money than they have, some less. This is something they will meet with all through life, so early experience in learning to make what they have go as far as possible will be all to the good. Some adults are forever bemoaning the fact that they can't "do as much" for their friends as the friends do for them. Real friendship isn't on a basis of "returns" for gifts or invitations or what not. Children should be taught that it is not so much what they can spend on their friends as what they give in the? way of loyalty, sympathy, and shared enjoyment that counts.

4. Learning about money should include becoming acquainted with family finances. The family that doesn't discuss the source of its money and how it's to be divided is probably a relic of the old days in which father held the purse strings. Nowadays he's pretty apt to hand them over to mother. She has more time for shopping than he does—or likes to better, whether it's for clothes or food.

That women do a very large share of the family buying is suggested by the immense amount of advertising addressed to them. But inquiry into family practices shows that parents tend to give boys far more worth-while experiences in managing money than girls. By age-old tradition boys are more often told about family resources and hear financial problems discussed more.

There are just as many ways open for preparing girls to know how to spend, save, lend, and borrow. Thoughtful effort put into such teaching would be one means by which girls could get practice on problems that will face them when they marry. Think of the needless wrangling over money that endangers the success of thousands of marriages—wrangling largely growing out of the ignorance of the marriage partners as to how to manage their money.

Girls of 10 or 12 can plan meals that are not only well balanced but also economical. They find it fun to be given money to cover a whole day's meals, provided an appreciative family praises the selections made. Shopping with mother, helping to judge the relative value of materials, and being given a voice in decisions about curtains, table linen, and clothes are valuable and enjoyable experiences. Study of mail-order catalogs and newspaper advertisements may be the basis for learning about comparative values and prices.

If 50-50 partnerships in marriage yield the best results—as studies indicate—why won't 50-50 partnerships between parents and their children lead their children into the same kind of satisfactory adult relationships? A father who lists for the children's benefit the taxes, rent and insurance he has to pay in a year and what he has to put aside to get the new car they all want, has the sympathetic understanding of his children. They are much more likely to appreciate their share of the family income if they understand where it comes from and where it goes to.

It gives children a sense of one-ness and family solidarity to be treated as responsible members of the group, who have a stake in everything that affects their parents.

If we think of the money we earn as belonging to the whole family, rather than as something doled out by us, everyone's feelings about it will be likely to be more wholesome. Money has come to mean so much in our lives only because fewer and fewer transactions can take place without it. In earlier days, even the younger members contributed to the family's livelihood. Boys tended the sheep from whose wool the girls knitted socks. The mother could feel a real partnership with her husband when she wove the flax he raised into sheets, or made soap and candles. Gradually we changed over to making money, instead of the things we now buy for money. This means we have to find other ways of giving all the family a feeling that they are still partners in the venture of family living.

5. Learning to save and to budget is an important part of money experience. Saving for things that are far in the future has no meaning to young children. Their goals must be close up, where they can reach them soon. To save for 3 weeks to buy a present for his mother seems just as tremendous an undertaking to a 6-year-old as saving in high school for college expenses seems to an adolescent. Failure to understand that little children cannot look very far ahead has discouraged many parents in their efforts to teach their children to save. Only as children mature are they able to set their sights on distant goals.

TO BE ABLE TO EARN RAISES A CHILD'S MORALE

6. Learning by earning is a very important part of children's experience. In our society children very early feel the urge to do things for which they get paid. The emphasis put on this kind of reward for accomplishment is contagious, and children catch it as they do measles.

It's difficult to take into account this very real need of children, and at the same time keep them from being too money-conscious. Some parents are afraid to pay children for performing duties

about the house; they hate, and rightly, to put services on a money basis that they feel should be given as a part of cooperative living.

If the family is really a unit, with every member having his share of responsibility, love, and security, there should be such a spirit of mutual helpfulness as to make any worry about such a possibility needless. Offering a child a nickel in order to get him to run an errand willingly is quite different from paying him for doing something outside his everyday jobs.

In every home there are "extra" things to do, things that have to be done seasonally, or that come irregularly, that give children chances to make a little money. The 8- or 9-year-old may have as his regular duties such things as bringing in the milk bottles and picking up his toys. But along comes a special need for money. "Can't I earn some?" he asks. Perhaps his mother has been putting off shining up her aluminum pans for lack of time. How about paying the child for this, or one of these many other things which we seldom get around to?

Children get a great lift out of having something to show for their efforts at an age when there are few if any ways open to them to earn money outside their homes. A little later, boys and girls can earn by taking care of neighbors' children, having newspaper routes, or, in the country, by raising a calf or chickens. But almost as early as children begin to have any use for money they also begin to want to earn some. The ingenious parent will think of many ways of giving children the thrill of earning little sums without endangering the child's willing cooperation when he is not paid for tasks.

Much will depend on the neighborhood in which a child lives as to how early he may begin to earn money by running errands, or mowing lawns. Children of 12 may not be strong or mature enough to undertake a newspaper route, but they are sometimes allowed to do so.

Every parent should do all he can to see that the spirit, as well as the letter, of child-labor laws is lived up to in his community. These laws help to protect children from situations they are not mature enough to cope with, and from being robbed of time needed for school, play, and family life.

SPECIAL PROBLEMS

1. An irregular income, varying greatly because of seasonal work or for other reasons sometimes makes allowances for chil dren difficult to manage.

Some families with irregular incomes say that they cannot set an amount which they can always have on hand to give out each week or month, according to the age of the child. Few children are so stupid as not to realize that their parents can't give them what they haven't got; the pinch of having the allowance reduced now and then is good preparation for the times in adult life when a higher cost of living or a salary reduction makes it necessary to reduce spending.

An irregular allowance may be used as a device for teaching saving. The fact that it is not often used in this way points out how poor the training of many adults in the use of money has been.

A wider application of a minimum yearly wage would make it easier for many families to give their children good practice in using money. Uncertainty and fear of want sometimes develop feelings of insecurity in children and help create penny-pinching and stingy habits, or the equally regrettable spending "while we have it."

2. Too much emphasis can be placed on money, of course. Children can become too concerned with whether or not they are getting "their share" if there is too much talk about dividing

the family income evenly. The more casual and matter-of-fact the attitude of the parents the less likely a child is to center his attention on himself.

3. Even while very young, children have very different attitudes toward money. One child may have many ideas as to how to spend what he gets, and be interested in saving only as it leads toward getting some much desired object. Another may seem to have very few cravings, and will take great pride in saving his money in order to have it hoarded up to talk about. Jane may be so stingy that she gives money toward a birthday present for her brother grudgingly, while her brother may be so generous that he seldom has a piece of candy left for himself.

A child who is unwilling to share or give shows by his actions that his relations with others are not comfortable. Gradually, he should be outgrowing the infantile self-centeredness that puts himself and his own interests first on all occasions. A school-age child who has no real appreciation of other people's wants has probably been catered to too much.

Another possible reason for a child's appearing "selfish" is that he is very insecure. He hangs on to his money because he dimly senses this is one means by which people gain personal security. The more friendless a person is, child or adult, the more likely he is to depend upon possessions to give him comfort. Money is such an important symbol of safety that even a child may get some comfort from possessing it. In such a case, some way must be found of making the child feel there's solid ground under him of understanding and love.

The opposite behavior, of giving too lavishly, really suggests a kind of insecurity, too. Offhand, it seems like a pleasing trait, but examined more closely, it sometimes turns out to be a child's effort to buy other people's liking. One wonders in such cases about the amount and quality of affection the youngster is getting at home.

14

Developing wholesome sex attitudes

"Let sleeping dogs lie" is often the attitude of parents when it comes to considering the sex education needs of the school child. "Time enough later on," we fool ourselves by saying. We push into the background something that we don't like to admit is really a concern right along.

PLANNING IS NECESSARY

More and more, though, thoughtful parents are undertaking wholeheartedly their obligation to make the matter of sex behavior, feelings, and understanding a part of their planned guidance of their children from the earliest years. They realize that failure to weave in this thread may weaken the whole fabric of their child's future life. By school age, a child's curiosity about his body, and about where babies come from has either been answered satisfactorily enough for the moment, or it has been crammed down into the realm of tabooed subjects.

Let's hope the first is true; but, in either case, the widening interests of the school-age child give us a good chance to do a quiet, natural job of satisfying his present needs and preparing him for the big changes of the teen age. If we are ourselves unsure or emotionally tense, our first step is to free ourselves of foolish fears or inhibitions.

This can be done. Parents have the strongest possible motive for learning to do so—their children's welfare. A motive or goal always makes learning easier, whether it's learning to sew, or typewrite, or swim. Illiterate men in the army learned to read and write in from 4 to 8 weeks, under pressure of their longing to keep in touch with their families. We can learn new, or more liberal, attitudes toward sex, because of a similar powerful motive—desire to be able to communicate freely with our children.

There are many good, simple books that can not only give us the necessary background of facts, but also help us to lift a veil and peer back into our own childhood. They help us to see how we came to entertain the feelings, good, bad, or indifferent, that we have attached to sex. Reading and study help, but discussion with others helps even more to free us and make us unafraid.

DO WE KNOW OUR CHILDREN?

First we may need information about what is going on in the child, who on the surface seems fairly indifferent to sex during these years. We may not see much evidence of sex interest, or activity that can be called sex activity, except as boys and girls tend to draw apart, and mingle less than before with the opposite sex. If very little interest is displayed, it is partly because children are quick to see that some things are not freely and openly discussed or done. For example, the practice of having separate toilets for boys and girls makes it obvious even to beginning school children that excretion is not only something private, but something each sex excludes the other from observing. By the time children go to school, their parents usually have begun to have boys and girls dress in different rooms, and the earlier habit of letting them take their baths together has been dropped. These, and dozens of other ways of behaving, so commonplace that we accept them without a thought, are such a part of a child's training in his home and his particular cultural group that he builds up sex awareness as he does a general feeling about sunshine and rain. His awareness can be wholesome and natural, like his enjoyment of sunshine, or tinged with disagreeable meaning. A "gloomy day feeling" about sex is not anything we want to encourage.

INFORMATION ISN'T ALL

We must not make the mistake of thinking that information is all a child needs. Really, that is probably the lesser part of our job. Although accurate and definite knowledge is highly desirable, the feelings a child builds up, the interpretation of the information he gets, will determine how he puts that information to use. Children get a good deal of sex-related information at school in all kinds of subjects. Our job is to see that their attitudes toward this whole matter remain wholesome.

We inject our feelings into our children, willy-nilly. If we hated and feared arithmetic in childhood, we'll have a different attitude toward Joan's struggles with long division than if we enjoyed it. So with sex. If we have feelings of disgust or fear about sex, we'll find those feelings creeping into our children's lives. This makes it of first importance for us to be sure that sex is a wholesome, constructive force in our own lives.

If a child's two parents have a good relationship based on real sympathy and understanding of each other's needs—sexual and otherwise—their unconscious influence will be the main food on which the child's adjustment feeds. Their frankness, their love for each other, will be the soil from which his attitudes and feelings spring.

Of course there are some basic facts that a child needs to be acquainted with, that we parents must give him, if he is to avoid being confused and troubled by misinformation such as we ourselves probably met with in childhood.

He needs to know how his body works, to understand the marvelous mechanism of his muscles, lungs, and heart and what happens to the food he eats. If he's given facts about how his body is nourished he can take the body wastes for granted and without disgust as being the unused elements of the food he eats and the water he drinks. He needs to know the names of the various parts of his body, their purpose, and a little bit about how they perform, from his intricate brain, through his digestive organs and genital system, down to the bony structure of his feet. He needs to know that there are hidden glands in his body, glands that don't open to the outside like his tear ducts, but manufacture and pass on their secretions inside the body at appropriate times, bringing about changes not only in his appearance but in his feelings, too.

He needs to know the reasons back of both the written and unwritten rules governing sex behavior: why marriage and family life are necessary for the protection and welfare of each oncoming generation; how and why it has come about that in our way of life, mating taking place as soon as sexual maturity is reached in the teens is considered undesirable; that only by putting off mating until the parents have become well enough established to give proper care to their children can children's safety and well-being be assured. When he understands all these things he can better accept the restraints that society imposes on him. A strong, harmonious relationship between his parents unconsciously influences a child to regard marriage with respect.

He needs to have the powerfulness of the sex urge that arises in adolescence explained; to understand how this strong drive is in itself neither good nor bad, but simply a necessity to the continuance of the race. Boys and girls need to learn how primitive sex behavior, from being originally a purely physical manifestation, has come to be associated in successful marriage with all that is highest and best in us. It is important for them to know that this has come about through the development of family life, and the devotion which the partners, first drawn together, perhaps, through the awakening of sex interest, come to feel for each other. Only by the building up of affection and shared interests and experiences has this become possible.

Especially as the time draws near when they will become mature sexually, at puberty, boys and girls need a clear, straightforward explanation of the ways they are going to change physically, and of how those bodily changes are going to be accompanied by emotional changes. Thousands of youngsters suf-

fer every year from not being given even the vaguest sort of help: the girl who is not prepared for menstruation, or for the changed interests she begins to feel; the boy whose voice begins to change, who surreptitiously tries his hand at shaving, and who worries needlessly about nocturnal emissions.

MATURATION RATES ARE DIFFERENT

Girls need explanations even earlier than boys for they mature earlier. (See physical growth, p. 174.) Often this doubles their puzzlement: they feel out of step, because they seem older than the boys of their age, and yet they are probably being surrounded by an increased amount of protection by their parents. Unless they are given an understanding of the meaning of menstruation they may be shocked and frightened at its first appearance. They need to know beforehand that menstruation is merely a device by which their body discards the blood, disintegrating tissue, and other materials the uterus stores up in its lining to nourish the egg which is released each month by the ovaries. That when, during the child-bearing years this egg is not fertilized by meeting with a sperm cell, it passes out of the body along with the blood that has lined the uterus in preparation for the possible nesting there of the egg. When this plain and commonsense explanation of menstruation is given, it can be accepted as a natural and normal function.

Girls need an explanation of the changes that are to come about in boys, too—just as boys need to know how girls mature. To learn of their own earlier maturation helps girls to see why they are often attracted to older boys, rather than to those of their own age. It helps to make plain to them their part in social life between the sexes to know that the male is more aggressive in sex behavior than the female, and that their behavior will have a lot to do with what they may expect from boys.

Once a boy has reached school age, it is often assumed that his father is a more suitable person to turn to for help than his mother. Fathers should be on such friendly terms with their sons as to make embarrassment or reserve unnecessary at any age. But some men seek to escape the responsibility for giving their sons sex information. Unless, or until, a father feels prepared to do so in an easy, natural way he probably should not attempt to handle his son's questions.

Because, in our way of life, mothers are usually closer to their young children through their day-in and day-out contacts, a boy's mother is perhaps more often the person who has given him answers all along, and to whom he has turned first for everything from a skinned knee to an explanation of death.

But she, never having been a boy, cannot possibly enter into his feelings the way his father can. Also if a child comes to rely solely on his mother, a valuable chance is lost for father-and-son contacts, and understanding. Boys need more, not fewer, such bonds. The ideal thing, of course, is for mother and father to be so in tune with each other and with their children that they can share this responsibility like any other; that whenever the occasion arises, discussion of this subject is as natural as talk about where coal comes from, or what causes the frost on a window.

As the physical and psychological changes associated with puberty begin to come about, though, there is a very real reason why a boy's father can handle questions better than his mother.

One of the most noticeable things about the youngster at such a time, boy or girl, is the new awareness of sex. The first way this may impress itself upon us is by our children's increasing modesty. They begin to insist on more privacy. The boy no longer wants his mother to come in and scrub his back when he takes a bath. The whole matter of sex is becoming infused with emotion. A boy's mother is no longer just his mother—she is a woman, too. There is a rising consciousness that the old love relationship between mother and son must alter, now that he is on his way to becoming a man.

Does it seem unnecessary to discuss here a situation that will not force its way into our attention until the teens? Though we are discussing children of 12 and under, what we will be up against later really has a very important bearing now. We don't need to put a stumbling block in our path. We can avoid doing so if we give children adequate preparation before the stage is reached when sex takes on a highly personal and emotional color. When such confidence and understanding exist in the preadolescent years, a child expects and is readier to meet the coming of puberty.

HOW THE SCHOOL CAN HELP

Of course, parents have the primary responsibility for the sex education of their children. There are some parents, though, who hate to face the fact that their children are going to grow up; who try to get out of hearing of the approaching sound of teen-age problems. But help must come from somewhere if the adolescent years are to be the pleasant time they should be.

If parents feel unable to do the job as it should be done, then they may want to see that the school (the only other agency that reaches all children) takes over some of this responsibility, and handles it according to the most approved methods. "A talk" to boys or girls by a physician, or someone pulled in because a serious need is suddenly felt, won't answer the purpose. Little can be said for such a separate and isolated "talk," even with the best of intentions on the part of all concerned. It lifts the subject out of its context of everyday life, and spotlights it, with resulting overemphasis. Both too little, and too much> is said. For one child, such an approach may be mildly amusing; another may have his curiosity stimulated. It is next to impossible to give in a single lecture information that will be useful to children from the great variety of backgrounds and of the degrees of maturity found in a single school grade.

If parents feel that sex education should be included in school guidance, they should find out what the most desirable methods are. To insert a course into the curriculum is not the answer. But with the cooperation of intelligent and personally well-adjusted teachers, the school can carry on a broad and pervasive program, where every single subject, from mathematics to art, contributes to an all around interpretation of what sex means in our lives.

Does it sound farfetched to say that mathematics can make a contribution? The right teacher can make it clear as daylight that figures and money are a part of family relations; that the conflicting needs of different family members, sometimes based on sex attitudes, are often responsible for misunderstandings about family budgeting and the fair distribution of money.

English classes can contribute through discussion of characters in stories and novels; social studies, by talking over the reasons for laws relating to children and marriage; biology can give background physical facts.

When both parents and schools arrive at the point where they are prepared to help children on their way to the goal of mental and emotional health through building wholesome sex attitudes we will have fewer tragedies in adult life.

15

Growth in middle childhood

Between early childhood and adolescence comes middle childhood, a time when physical growth jogs along at a pretty even pace, without the rapid gains that came earlier and will come again later. It is a period when parents can breathe a sigh of relief, too, for it is a relatively safe and healthy period. The time when the childhood diseases are most dangerous is past. Colds, broken arms and legs, and infections are bothersome, but parents put in fewer anxious days and nights over sickness than they did when their children were younger. Even the accident rate for this age group is strikingly lower than for others. It is less than half as high as for the under 5's and those between the ages of 15 and 24. (See health care, p. 177.) This "breathing spell" between the rapid growth periods of childhood and adolescence enables parents to get off on the right foot before the coming of the teens brings a whole new range of concerns.

It is a time when a child is all set for a great deal of learning. His mind is on the stretch. He can grasp many kinds of new ideas. He is very able physically. His muscles are well controlled, so that he can become skilled in a great variety of physical activities, such as swimming, milking a cow, playing a musical instrument, or batting a ball.

What is going on with respect to growth and how does it affect our handling of the child? For one thing, body build differences that may have been hidden by chubbiness while children were little begin to show up. Characteristic family tendencies toward broadness and stockiness or slenderness with accompanying long bones now become apparent.

HEIGHT AND WEIGHT

In judging children's growth we must consider the great differences in children's types. So much depends upon biological and family background that it is useless to compare a child with another of his age, to see if he is growing properly. Instead, we need to compare him with himself, at an earlier period, or with other children who resemble him in general body type. There are slender, narrowly built children, and broader, thicker children; children who are small-boned and children who are large-boned. There are those who will always be "big for their age," others will always seem small, though this lack of conformity k right for them. Children who are tall when young keep right on being tall for their age, with temporary exceptions.

Growth in weight does not follow as regular a pattern as in ¼eight, because of the many things that influence it, such as illnesses, the presence or absence of nourishing foods, and of emotional conditions that affect a child's well-being. Because these are things over which his parents have a good deal of control, a child's gains in weight should be watched more closely than his gains in height. What he eats while he is growing will be used first for his immediate energy needs, and next for growth in length, for his bony development. What he adds in flesh will be an individual matter of his having the right foods and other conditions, like happiness, that contribute to good nutrition. The kind of weight a child puts on is important; a child may look comparatively thin, but have excellently developed muscles. Another may be fat without being well-nourished. In general, children add about five pounds a year in weight during this period.

Girls are, from birth up to about the age of 9 or 10, both shorter and lighter than boys. From about 10 to 14 or 15, however, this is reversed, as girls begin their preadolescent spurt in height and weight earlier than boys. Then the boys get ahead again, and stay there.

At every age girls are more mature than boys. Their teeth appear earlier, their organs mature more rapidly, and the endocrine changes that make them into adolescents start earlier. By age 12 they are about 2 years ahead of boys in general development. The effects these differences have on social adjustment are discussed elsewhere (see p. 164).

BODY PROPORTIONS

The parts of the body do not grow evenly and regularly. Each has its own growth pattern. Some parts are much larger in proportion than others, from the earliest years. At 6, the head is about as large as it ever will be. At this time it makes up about one-sixth of the entire body length, while in adulthood its proportion is one eighth of the body length, the difference in proportion being made up mostly by the greater growth of the legs. The trunk of the body is long in proportion to the arms and legs. The latter, especially the legs, have a lot of growing to do, as they are relatively short in early life.

The nervous system, of which the brain makes up the largest part, grows very rapidly at first, slows down decidedly by the age of 6, and is about completed by the end of the period we are concerned with. Just the opposite is true of the genital organs, which grow very little during the years from 6 to 12, but begin to speed up rapidly during the teens. Only one part of the body is strikingly more developed now than later, the lymph glands, which gradually subside during adolescence. This partly explains the great frequency of enlarged tonsils and adenoids in early middle childhood.

MUSCLES, BONES, AND TEETH

Children's muscles are developing rapidly during the school years. Evidence of this is the popularity of strength-testing feats, and the skills that take bodily endurance. By the age of 12, well over a third of the body weight is due to muscle tissue.

The bony growth of children is very interesting, although it is so well hidden that we seldom give much thought to it. The development of bones that underlies changes in size is brought about by a gradual shift from soft, cartilaginous tissues to firm and hard, or ossified, structures. The bones both support and protect. They form the framework of the body, and are bound together by the muscles. Bones grow both in thickness and at the ends, where cartilage is being gradually added and calcification, or hardening, goes on. A child's body contains more separate bones than an adult's, for bones fuse together as growth proceeds.

The greater softness of children's bones means that their bodies are more flexible than adults', which has both advantages and disadvantages. Children can make movements impossible to grownups, but the lack of firmness in their bones means that care must be taken to see that pressure does not cause deformed bones. The reason we hear so much about providing well-shaped shoes that are large enough to allow room for the growth of the feet is because a child's foot bones may be permanently harmed by being crowded into short or narrow shoes that distort the bones, Even the pressure due to short stockings is bad. Those children are fortunate who live where they can go barefoot safely.

For the same reason good posture is of immense importance. Children and young adolescents should not do manual work that means using the same set of muscles for long periods. Many of the jobs that children do, like transplanting and weeding, cramp and strain the body. They prevent its free use as a whole, so necessary while bone growth is going on.

Poor habits of sitting while reading or studying, with the shoulders bent; bad ways of standing, so that one hip or shoulder is higher than the other; sleeping slumped into awkward positions because of a poor mattress or bedspring, all these things should be prevented. Children's beds should be selected with great care. They should have firm mattresses and good springs. Children should never sleep on makeshift beds, or use old ones relegated to the children's rooms because they are not good enough for adults.

Extreme fatigue has a very bad effect on body posture; a child's need of frequent rest, change of position, and exercise of the whole body is plain to be seen. The "activity program" in modern schools is an attempt to meet these needs among others.

To understand what is going on in the child's bones we need only look at X-ray pictures of the way the bones change from year to year. From having in infancy no bones in the wrist hard enough to show up by X-ray, a child develops a large number of bones by the age of 9, and these will harden and fuse together as he becomes more mature. The same process is going on in other parts of the body, as well.

The development of the bony part of the child's body is closely connected with his general physiological maturity, which means that of all his organs. Not until children reach the "right" age of skeletal development do they become sexually mature. Thus, a girl who menstruates early, by 11 or 12, will also be found to have reached a greater "skeletal age" than the majority of girls of her chronological age. Children who are large and well-developed are likely also to be well-advanced in their bony development.

The teeth are, of course, part of the bony structure of the body, and are important both to a child's health and his appearance. We need a great deal more knowledge about the teeth, and how to keep them from decaying. However, if we did as well as we know how to do, at the present stage of our knowledge, we would be able to boast of progress far beyond what we are making.

We have long known the importance of the sixth-year molars, but we still let these four teeth become diseased or decayed in the mouths of thousands upon thousands of children because we have not all realized that these are not "baby" but permanent teeth. They often come in before any of the baby teeth fall out, and their importance in the jaw as the guides that determine the position of the later-coming teeth goes unnoticed. Even the teeth that drop out, and so are called "deciduous," are important enough to warrant being carefully cared for and filled. If they decay and are pulled long before the new teeth push to the surface of the jaw, these latter teeth may not come in straight because the shape of the jaw has been affected.

As the permanent teeth are forming in the jaw long before they erupt, the child's diet must contain plenty of good building material, especially phosphorus and calcium, and the vitamins (see nutrition, p. 181). Because the phosphorus and calcium in foods cannot be utilized by the body unless vitamin D is also present, the use of fish liver oil should be continued during the growing years. Foods that give much exercise to the jaws, that have to be well chewed, are helpful to jaw development. It is almost impossible to find tooth decay among the older natives on the Pribilof Islands, and very easy to find it among their children, who have been introduced to our soft, ready-prepared foods and sweets.

There are great individual differences in children as to the age when their permanent teeth erupt. Also, girls' come earlier than boys'. By the age of 8 or 9, most children have 10 or 11 permanent teeth. By the time they are 10 and 11 they acquire 14 to 16 of their second teeth. But by the age of 12, most children have their full set of teeth, with the exception of the wisdom teeth that appear in very late adolescence. If there is a tendency for the teeth to be crowded (impacted) the wisdom teeth may cause trouble when they come in.

When the upper and lower jaws do not grow evenly, so-called "malocclusion" or poor fitting together of the upper and lower teeth may happen. There are occasional cases where the teeth are so irregular that chewing is interfered with, which in turn affects nutrition. If either the lower or upper jaw tends to stick out because the lower teeth overlap the upper in front or the upper teeth protrude too far beyond the lower, the child should be examined frequently by a dentist specially trained in this field, known as orthodontia. Sometimes the condition will correct itself as the child grows; in other cases it may be necessary to have special treatment in order that a child's appearance may be improved. Before the jaw has become completely calcified this is a fairly easy procedure; later on, little or nothing can be done.

The contours of the face change quite appreciably during adolescence, when the features take on their adult proportions. Then the nose may not be so prominent or the forehead so rounded. Many a child who has disapproved of his profile finds it changing for the better. But when a child between 6 and 12 has a chin that recedes noticeably, or lips that cannot be closed because of protruding teeth, no pains should be spared to make him feel happier about his appearance, even though this may mean rather long-drawn-out orthodontia. If it is an expense his family can't afford, effort should be made to find a clinic that does such work free. The discomfort and the conspicuous-ness of braces are in many cases offset by the child's feeling that the end results will be worth while.

Although some children with the best of diets have poor teeth, it is still worth while to provide foods that are known tooth-builders. To some extent, good and poor teeth seem to run in families. Until more is known, we cannot insure a child's having good teeth by feeding him the "right" foods, having him brush his teeth, and go to a dentist regularly. But these things undoubtedly help.

SPECIAL FEATURES OF GROWTH

Because girls go through their preadolescent spurt in growth earlier than boys, many of the girls begin to approach their full height by the age of 12 or 13, the twelfth year being the period during which most girls gain the most in both weight and height. Among the first parts of the body to reach adult size are the hands and feet. The girl of 13 may be startled to find herself having to buy shoes that are as large as or even larger than her mother's. She will take comfort in knowing that her body will "grow up" to her hands and feet. Many older boys and girls would have been saved a lot of distress if some one had taken pains to explain to them the unevenness of growth that makes them feel awkward and conspicuous. A 12-year-old girl who is taller than any of the boys in her room at school needs to be reassured that in 2 or 3 years' time she will not seem so tall, because they will have caught up to her. Boys and girls who go through a stage of being extra plump need to be told that this will pass, and that a few years hence they may be among the more slender of their age group.

When a child is unusually tall and promises always to be so, he may be made *to* feel pride in his height by a tactful buildup of the advantages of being tall. The father of one very tall girl always took pains to point out any tall woman they saw who dressed tastefully and carried herself well. The girl, impressed by her father's admiration for tall women, was glad she was going to be one.

Of course many a girl who reaches her full height early will not seem tall later on, when the slower-maturing girls catch up to her. It is well to remember this, and reassure the girl who for a while outstrips her classmates, who are near her in age.

Although smallness goes with the femininity often thought of as an asset in women, girls who are short hate to have their smallness remarked on. It would be a good idea for both parents and teachers to keep from making personal remarks about children's variations in either height or weight. The small-for-his-age boy may be worried for fear he will always be short. This is not likely to be a matter of much concern in the 6 to 12 group, because so few boys will yet have begun to grow fast. But there will be an occasional small boy who, judging by family tendencies, will probably remain relatively small, whatever his age. In view of the many ways in which some short men try to make up for being decidedly below the average in height, it is just as well to think about this boy's problem well ahead of time, and try to see that he has many sources of satisfaction to offset this limiting feature. Just as it makes a child self-conscious to have constant comments made on how much he has grown, so it brings on worry and feelings of inadequacy to be reminded of his small size. If he has skills or gifts that lie can be proud

of he will have less time to spend bemoaning his shortness. In most cases, of course, even boys who have been small through their elementary school years make such quick strides in growth in the teens that by the time they are 16 or 17 they have forgotten that they ever were worried about their height. However, this is one of the big secret fears of many young boys.

PREPUBERTAL CHANGES

Few boys show signs of approaching puberty by the age of 12, but quite a number of girls will give evidence of coming sexual maturity. The development of the breasts and calves of the legs is one of the more obvious evidences. A widening of the pelvis is going on, too, preparing the girl for child-bearing later.

The tendency toward a slightly earlier age of menstruation, observed nowadays, is presumed to be related to the better nutrition of children in recent years.

Sex differences in strength, endurance, and motor ability are less marked from 6 to 12 than later, but girls are already beginning to show that they are less adapted to athletic types of activity. The physical endurance of girls is less than that of boys. They tire more easily, and take longer to recover from the effects of physical exertion like running. By the age of 14 or 15 girls have reached the limit of their gains in motor performance, although there are great differences, of course, between individual girls. A "boyish" type of build has some influence on a girl's physical prowess.

The amount of encouragement and practice children have strongly affects their use of their bodies in activity. A girl who is not urged to learn bodily skills during middle childhood is less and less likely to learn them as she gets older. Not only does motor performance begin to decline in the teens but social attitudes do not stress athletic games and feats for girls. But girls who have early become enthusiastic about sports often go on to remarkable achievement. Learning to figure-skate, to play tennis or volley ball, to ride or to swim must come at a time when enthusiasm for physical activity is high if girls are to make full use of their physical powers.

16

Keeping your child healthy

The grade-school years are a comparatively healthy period in a child's life, but there are still enormous improvements to be made in the care children get in these years. We are constantly adding to our knowledge about how to have well-nourished children, but somehow we do not manage to get this knowledge put into practice very fast. Information about how to prevent rickets, for example, has greatly cut down the number of children who have rickets, but the nutrition of our children is still far from being good.

Nutrition is affected by every part of a child's life: his food, his sleep, his activity, his state of mind. A child cannot really be said to be well-nourished unless all these things are taken care of.

Malnutrition is one of the most common and often one of the least easily recognized obstacles to health. People rarely think of irritability as being a symptom of a poorly balanced or inadequate diet. Because fatigue is a feeling everyone knows, we tend to pass it over as of little consequence, when it may point to a nutritional lack that could be remedied. Again, malnutrition is often thought of as something that refers to food lacks alone, because we associate "nourishment" with food. Actually, a child who is malnourished may be getting plenty of good food, but not the active outdoor play, or the sunlight, or the fun out of life that puts his food to work for him. Infection somewhere in his body may be dragging a child down. Irregularity of meals, so that a child "pieces" in between, may be responsible in families which are careless about when mealtimes come. Late hours, or too little sleep, may play a part in mal-nourishment. A child whose life is on a hit-or-miss basis may never be very hungry. Poor sleeping conditions may mean that although a child is spending enough time in bed, he is not getting a good quality of sleep, because of poor ventilation, overcrowding, or noise. A school-age child may have extremely poor eating habits because too much attention is paid to his food whims; perhaps he eats too much of certain things, like cookies or crackers, to the exclusion of other very necessary ones.

Surveys of the breakfasts eaten by school children reveal that a large number of them start off to school very poorly fortified to begin the day's activities. A good many eat no breakfast at all. Often these same children have very poor lunches. Whether lunch is carried from home, or provided at school, the child seldom gets enough of the foods of which two or three servings a day are desirable, such as vegetables and fruits.

Because so many children eat lunch away from home, dinner is often the only really good meal of their day. They can hardly make up in one meal, even if very well planned, for the lacks of two others.

STARTING THE DAY RIGHT

Many failures to eat a good breakfast can be blamed on hurry. Haste to get off to school implies the child stayed in bed until the very last minute which pushes the blame back on the time he got to bed the night before.

Sometimes the child's anxiety about getting off to school on time points to pressure that is put on him in school. When a child must catch a bus, or meet a car-pool, his mother must see that he is up in time so that he does not feel too hurried to eat a good breakfast.

Children in the early grades do not have a clear idea of time. It will not help to keep saying "Hurry, hurry!" but it will help to have a schedule laid out for getting off to school on time. Planning the night before what is to be worn, fixing lost buttons or rips, being sure that caps, mittens, and school materials are in their proper places will be a big help. Scheduling turns at the bathroom or sink, having breakfast ready on the table, and remembering to allow time for toothbrushing and a bowel movement after breakfast are seemingly trivial but important steps in the morning activities.

If, when care is taken to see that plenty of time is allowed for all the necessary details, the child still seems nervous and ill at ease, his mother ought to consult with his teacher to make sure that too much emphasis is not being placed on his not being tardy. Worry has no place in the life of a child.

The habits of the older members of the family have much to do with children's attitudes about meals. If late-rising makes the whole family feel rushed, so that everyone eats breakfast on the run, children will follow this same pattern.

Many children of the 6-to-12 group spend the whole school day away from home. Even where there is a well-planned school lunch, and this is an essential, many children may spend part of their lunch money foolishly at a corner grocery or drug store. Candy and soft drinks, if indulged in at the expense of more desirable foods, can do much to upset a carefully planned home diet. This is not to say that all buying of such things need be forbidden; school children are so active that they can take care of some extra energy-producing material.

Not until children are in their teens do they begin to feel any real interest in health, and then it is because it affects their appearance rather than for its own sake. But much earlier *habit* can begin to play a part, and this is where parents come in. They have the very best opportunity to set up good health habits in their children by always providing suitable foods. Few habits are stronger than those connected with food. Parents have a pretty free hand in setting up eating patterns in their own families; they mostly have themselves to blame if they fail to bring about, wholesome eating habits.

When lunch is provided at school, some attention must be paid to guiding children's choice of foods. They can be encouraged to take the plate lunch, if one is provided; or if not, to take a vegetable, as well as a main dish and dessert. Mothers who take an interest in the school lunch can often make changes for the better in the type of food provided; by observing children's choices they can learn how color, texture, and the attractiveness with which food is served influence children's selection. By asking a child what he had at noon we can avoid serving the same vegetable that night, perhaps, and, at the same time, keep track unobtrusively of whether he is eating wisely at school.

One way to prevent children from craving sweets at unsuitable times is to make sure that they are supplied at home at mealtimes with raisins, figs, dates, apples, fruit juices, and other things that renew their energy.

FOOD NEEDS

While school-age children can eat the general family diet, with the exception of tea and coffee, their mothers need to keep an eye out to see that they do not eat too much of some kinds of food, and too little of others.

Most children like the foods that are good for them: bread and butter, milk, fruit, vegetables, and meat. But in case a child has become finicky about his eating, school entrance is a good time to make a fresh start. His school, in its health teaching, will reinforce our efforts—in the beginning grades children are very much impressed by what teacher says. One little boy came home accusing his mother of not serving as many vegetables daily as his teacher said were necessary. For days he suspiciously counted to make sure his mother was living up to what he had learned she ought to provide.

If at this period desirable eating habits don't get to be a matter of course, it will be harder to establish them. As time goes on the child will eat away from home more often so it is essential that we know he can be depended on to eat a sufficient variety and suitable amounts of foods for both energy and body building.

If a period of rapid growth sets in before the age of 12, as it so often does in the case of girls, it may be necessary to check up to see that added growth needs are being taken care of. A girl at this age is prone to eat extra cookies, candy, or ice-

cream sodas when she's hungry. As these take care of extra energy needs only, they must not crowd out those more necessary foods for which the need goes up sharply at this time.

Following are foods that contribute to children's needs by supplying energy and providing materials for body building and maintenance. They are called "The Basic Seven Food Groups."

DAILY FOOD NEEDS

Each of the seven should be included in every day's meals.

Group 1

Dark green, leafy, and deep yellow vegetables-

Such as broccoli, kale, green peppers, turnip and other greens, carrots, sweet potatoes, winter squash.

Raw, cooked, frozen, canned.

One or more servings daily.

Group 2

Citrus fruit, tomatoes, raw cabbage and other high vitamin C foods- Such as oranges, grapefruit, lemons, limes, tomatoes, musk-melons, pineapples, strawberries; raw cabbage, green peppers, and turnips. (If fruits are hard to get, use more, especially raw, from groups 1 and 3.)

One or more servings daily.

Group 3
Potatoes and other vegetables and fruit-Such as potatoes, beets, celery, corn, eggplant, lettuce, mushrooms, rutabagas, summer squash; apples, apricots, peaches, pears, rhubarb, prunes, raisins, dates, figs, and other fruits and berries.
Raw, cooked, frozen, canned, dried.
Two or more servings daily.

Group 4
Milk, cheese, ice cream.
Milk—whole, skim, evaporated, condensed, dried, buttermilk.
Three to 4 cups daily.
The following portions contain as much calcium as a cup of milk: 1 ounce cheddar cheese, 4 ounces cream cheese, 12 ounces cottage cheese, 2 or 3 large dips of ice cream.

Group 5
Meat, poultry, fish, eggs, dried beans and peas, nuts.
One serving of meat or fish daily if possible. Four or more eggs a week.
Two or more servings a week of nuts, peanut butter, or dried beans or peas.

Group 6
Bread and cereals. Whole grain or enriched and restored every day.

Group 7
Butter or fortified margarine daily.
Energy foods (such as rice, jams and jellies, cakes, candy, bacon and salad oils) may be used in addition to the 7 basic foods, but should not be used in place of them. Reasons for continuing the use of fish-liver oil through these years are given on p. 173.

School-age children are constantly on the go. They often need extra food between meals. If a child's appetite for his meals is hearty, and he eats the necessary variety, he should be his own judge of the amount of extra food he needs.

The main point to remember about between-meal eating is that it should be regular, not just "piecing" any time a child feels like it. A lunch of sandwiches and milk or fruit eaten right after school, or in the middle of the morning should not keep a child from being hungry for his next meal. Without a reminder from his mother, a child may wait until too close to the next meal hour to make lunching desirable.

UNDERWEIGHT AND OVERWEIGHT

The child whose parents have been told by their doctor that he needs to put on weight may not be able to eat any larger amounts of food than he has been eating. He needs more of the highly concentrated foods, such as eggs (if he tolerates them well), cream, and butter. Evaporated milk, used in cooking without being diluted, adds to the nourishment in soups or puddings. More butter or margarine on his bread, more cream on his cereal may be used.

The fats, starches, and milk in his diet can be increased only if they agree with him; they should not be added too rapidly, nor should they crowd out valuable foods like vegetables and fruits.

Often the underweight child needs extra rest just as much as he needs extra food. He may be a child who is overactive and easily overstimulated. More careful supervision of his play may help. Providing interesting, quiet occupations will keep him from feeling so thwarted if he must cut down on active, romping play. If he must rest before meals and go to bed earlier than his playmates, he may be furnished with books or quiet table games or a radio in his room.

The long, lean type of child is sometimes assumed to be underweight when he is really in good physical condition.

No attempt should be made to reduce the weight of a child except upon the advice of a competent physician. If a diet is suggested, great care should be taken to see that it includes enough bulk (supplied by vegetables and fruits) and the essential vitamins and minerals that keep the body in good repair. Unlike the underweight child, who needs more fats and starchy foods, the overweight child may need careful supervision to see that he does not overdo such items as butter, cream, cake and candy.

A fat child's problem will not always be solved by attention to his diet. Some children overeat because, in the absence of other satisfactions, they have a craving for pleasure, and eating is an easy way to get some. A child who is ignored by other children, whose home life is unhappy, or who for any other reason feels wretched may turn to greedy gobbling of food, as another turns to daydreams.

Overweight caused by lack of glandular balance is another matter. The physician who takes care of the child will try to determine whether the cause is physical or psychological.

GOOD CONDITIONS FOR EATING

To get the most benefit from their food children need to eat under pleasant conditions. They need to be relaxed and at ease if digestion is to be good. Because the school-age child is typically in a rush, it is often a good idea to set a definite length of time which must be spent at the table, say 15 or 20 minutes at least. If this is a rule the urge to bolt his food and run back to play or school will be less, and nagging can be avoided.

The conscientious child is often worried for fear he may be late to school, which makes it important to have lunch, as well as breakfast, served in time so that the child will not feel hurried.

Since excitement of any kind—anger, fear, or any intense emotion—hinders digestion, parents should strive for a pleasant atmosphere at meals. *Meals are not the time to talk about a child's faults or to bring up disagreeable topics.* Harping on table manners may have an opposite effect to the desired one. If the table is neatly prepared, the food appetizingly served, and the parents' own table manners good, children will gradually, by imitation, learn a great deal about pleasing manners.

A few families still consider that the adults' conversation is all that matters at the family meals; others go to the extreme of letting children be the center of attention. If children are to learn to talk well they need to have a part in what goes on; but they need also to learn how to listen, and not to interrupt continually. They will be helped in learning how to be hospitable, and they will enjoy their meals more if their friends occasionally share them.

CARE OF THE TEETH

The state of a child's teeth is easier to determine than that of his nutrition, for defects in teeth can be seen. The percentage of school-age children having dental caries

or decay goes up steadily through the elementary-school years, running up into SO and 90 percent in different communities by age 12. The provision of a well-balanced diet, with plenty of the so-called protective foods, is probably the best means of prevention within parents' control. Because there seems to be a connection between sound teeth and the presence of fluorine in the water used for drinking, experiments are being made in applying fluorine to the teeth of children as a preventive measure.

Even when school examinations show that children's teeth are in poor condition, parents are often slow to have defects taken care of. Some of this failure is because parents are unable to pay for dental work, but a large share of it is simply neglect. It reflects the ignorance among parents themselves of the importance of a healthy mouth to over-all good health.

The sixth-year molars (so-called because they usually appear in that year) are especially likely to decay, and need very careful watching. Few adults have perfect sixth-year molars, which is silent evidence of neglect during childhood. This neglect is often the result of very early food lacks, due to parents' failure to know that these four molars are permanent teeth, and have been present in the child's jaw since before birth.

Since perhaps only 1 out of 10 school children pays any attention at all to the connection between health and good habits of eating, exercise, and rest, it is up to parents to supervise closely their children's habits in this period. Even though children may *know* that eating candy between meals is undesirable, they can't be depended on not to indulge. Health teaching in school needs to be bolstered up by whatever means parents can devise at home. Visual education seems to work better than talking about health needs, and parents might very well make more use of pictures, charts, and any other way they can to let their children *see* for themselves why healthy teeth are so important.

Parents would think a long while before they would deliberately do anything to prevent their children from having the best of health in adult life. And yet that is almost exactly what they do when they don't make two visits a year to the dentist or a dental clinic.

THE CHILD'S HEARING

The kind of hearing a child will have in adult life depends to some extent upon the care his ears get in childhood. It is not possible later on to make up for any neglect that occurred while the child was little, and early recognition of any existing trouble may help to keep hearing from becoming steadily worse.

Almost every kind of deafness seen in adults is found in children between 8 and 14 years old, with this difference: in children the impairment of hearing is just beginning, and it may be possible to prevent its progress.

Prevention of any hearing loss, of course, is better still. This means that great care should be taken when children have diseases such as measles, one very frequently associated with ear infections. Running ears, which if neglected may result in deafness, are often caused by chronic, or long continuing, infection in the tonsils and adenoids. Pain in the ear should never be "home treated" but a doctor or clinic should be visited. Colds—the main cause of absences from grade school—are one of the worst offenders in bringing about earache and the ear trouble that follows. The pity of it is that we take "colds" so casually. "It's just a cold" will never be the attitude of the mother who is truly interested in promoting her child's health, with special thought for his hearing.

One of the serious and immediate results of impaired hearing is the slowing up in school that is likely to result. One study showed that half of those children who are hard-of-hear-ing may be expected to be a grade behind, if they have not learned lip reading. Early discovery of any loss of hearing could keep this from happening.

THE CHILD'S EYESIGHT

Even though a child has had regular care by a physician up to the time he enters school, the chances are great that he has not had his vision tested or his hearing; relatively few physicians make a practice of doing this. Many schools now routinely test children's eyes, but with so many children to examine it *is* not always possible to do more than pick out those children whose eyes have rather obvious defects.

If a child holds his book close to his face; if he tips his head to odd angles when working; if he has sties frequently, or any discharge or redness about the eyes; if he squints; if he seems to have difficulty seeing things at any distance, his parents should have his eyes examined by a competent ophthalmologist —a physician who is an eye specialist.

Children sometimes are well along in the grades before any-one notices that their eyesight is poor. The child himself, of course, has no way of knowing that his eyes are not like other people's, and so may struggle along, though very much handi-capped. His parents are the ones who should be on the alert to rule out any such happening. They should give special thought to this when their child goes to school, and begins to use his eyes for close work more than he has before. Being on the lookout will make possible the early finding and correction of such things as near- or far-sightedness, astigmatism, or crossed eyes.

When study of a child's eyes reveals that he must wear glasses, parents should follow the eye doctor's recommendations closely as to how often follow-up examinations and change of glasses are needed. Because children's eyes are changing and developing rapidly, often new glasses are needed every year.

IMPORTANCE OF SLEEP AND REST

By the time children go to school they are usually sleeping about 11 hours out of the 24. From this time on, their constant cry is to be allowed to stay up later.

While there can be a very gradual decrease for the next few years in the length of time a child sleeps, no hard-and-fast rules can be given as to the exact amount needed at any given age, because each child's requirements are different. Just as some children thrive on less food than others, so children differ very decidedly in the amount of sleep necessary to their best health. A good general rule is to see to it that a school-age child goes to sleep early enough to awaken naturally in the morning. A little experimentation will determine whether being allowed up an extra 15 or 20 minutes at night means "dopey" irritability in the morning.

The older children grow the more varied and demanding interests they have, and the more independent they like to feel. If they have a hand in working out plans, they feel much less thwarted than when rules are laid down—with no back-talk, no discussion. But the last word must remain with the parents in matters of health. Twelve-year-old Mary may be so conscientious about home work that she wants to keep on with it after the agreed-upon hour for bedtime. Better than allowing her to talk us into letting her stay up till 10 "just this once" (which it never turns out to be) is a firm but sympathetic "no," and then later a conference with the teacher or teachers (after consulting with Mary) to find out just how much time she is expected to spend on home work. If a junior high-school child is overburdened with home work because teachers are making assignments without consulting each other, as occasionally happens, parent-school sifting out of the matter is the answer.

Whenever the prepubescent growth spurt sets in, which may very well happen before the teens in the case of girls, more rest and sleep are necessary. Growth makes great demands upon the body, which can be met only by ample sleep and food that contributes to body building. The easy tears and fits of temper that mothers frequently complain of in their daughters at the approach of adolescence are just as likely to be connected with unsatisfied sleep or food needs, as with glandular changes.

INTERFERENCES WITH SLEEP

Radio, television, and the movies give us and our children much pleasure nowadays but also cause some of our biggest headaches. They contribute immensely to our lives, but they also offer some perplexing health problems.

We know that children should have a chance to calm down at the end of the day, and yet that is just the time that they want to listen to the radio or go to a movie. Is it harmful to let them?

Careful study has shown that even after very mildly exciting movies, children's sleep is disturbed. The more thrilling the movie the greater the effect on the sleep. The disturbance is not just for a single night, but can be noted for 2 or 3 weeks. Children of the 6 to 12 ages are more affected by scenes of danger, and as they like hair-raising movies rather than romantic ones, these are the ones they'll pick out, if given a choice.

It stands to reason that the movies children see should be carefully selected. One reason is that they remember things that impress them on the screen so much longer than grown-ups do. They take seriously what slips off our minds in a twinkling. Sensitive children, who tend to have bad dreams or fears as a result of what they see on the screen, should, of course, be limited to pictures that are not frightening.

Even for children who seem to take excitement in their stride, week-night movies—even the "early show"—are not advisable during the school year. For nervous children an occasional daytime movie, of a mild type, is all that can be recommended. Lists of suitable movies are given each month in magazines on family life.

Television is harder to deal with than the movie. The parent who says, "It can always be turned off!" is forgetting that for a school-age child, to be doing, hearing, and seeing the same things his friends are is very important. His carefully protected health is of little use to him if he is "different" from his mates.

However, children whose parents have been firm and consistent from the beginning of their training come to accept a sensible bedtime matter-of-factly. Letting a child stay up a little later occasionally for a program he very much wants to hear, or when "special" company comes, will keep him from feeling that his parents enjoy putting obstacles between him and his pleasures.

ACCIDENT PREVENTION

More school-age children die every year from accidents than from appendicitis, heart disease, and pneumonia (the next most frequent causes of death) put together. As we all know, children of these ages are exposed to many more risks than more closely watched over younger children. Apparently we are doing a very poor job of teaching them how to avoid danger, when deaths from accidents are so high.

First in number come deaths from motor-vehicle accidents. Far below this, but next in order, come deaths by drowning, with many more boys being drowned than girls. Other causes of fatal accidents among children are burns, conflagration, injury by fall, and, among the older children, injury by firearms.

We have succeeded in greatly cutting down deaths from acute infectious disease and from tuberculosis, but have hardly reduced the fatalities from accidents at all.

What can parents do to cut down this unnecessary death toll?

1. They can take steps to see that their children have safer places to play. In some cities, for example, parents have insisted upon the roping off of certain streets for sliding, so there is no danger of sleds colliding with cars. Parents can work for more playgrounds, where children can run, climb, and jump in safety. They can make their own yards attractive by putting up parallel bars and swings, letting children build shacks, play basketball and croquet.

2. They can do a better job of teaching children to obey traffic rules. (This is something the average adult is very lax about himself.) Example and practice help more than harping on dangers.

3. They can see that their children learn how to swim (almost every city YM and YWCA gives lessons); that they understand such things as the danger of diving in shallow water, and learn how to give lifesaving aid. They can work for good supervision of swimming pools and lake shores.

4. They can teach the proper use of guns. This is an obliga tion some parents don't take seriously. They may refuse to let their children have a BB gun, in the mistaken notion that this will prevent accidents. Forbidding a boy to use a gun doesn't lessen his eagerness to do so. He will probably have opportuni-

ties—away from home and away from careful instruction—to handle guns. The temptation is great, and the risk of accident increases with the child's unfamiliarity with dangerous weapons.

A better plan is for a father to see to it that his boys—and girls too, if they want to—have practice in handling guns under his careful guidance. Begin when the child is little by teaching him never to point even a toy gun at a person. Fathers can teach marksmanship under safe conditions; how to carry a gun; how to get under or over a fence with one; how to get into and out of a boat safely while hunting. They can give an unfailing example of the importance of not leaving a loaded gun lying around.

5. They can teach children to be thoughtful and alert and to exercise judgment. That so many more boys than girls lose their lives in motor-vehicle accidents, by drowning and by shooting, highlights the far greater freedom that boys are allowed—without regard for the danger involved. Boys seem naturally somewhat more active and daring than girls; but this tendency is only part of the picture. Because they are active, bold, daring, it seems taken for granted that boys can take care of themselves. In the modern world dangers have increased without any increase whatever in our ability to look out for ourselves. Guns, heavy trucks, electricity, motorcycles are only a few of the dangerous things that are commonplace in our lives. They make it imperative for parents to teach children to keep a sharp look-out, and to give them opportunities for learning motor skills, and to use good judgment. The answer to the dangers of bicycle riding is not to refuse to let a child have a bicycle, but to see that he has a chance to learn to ride under safe conditions. We can extend his privileges about where he may ride as he gives evidence of taking precautions.

It would be a mistake to make children fearful or overcautious, which may be the result if parents hedge their children around with too much protection. Keeping children from doing things is not the answer in accident prevention; rather, they should have practical safe experience in doing many things, so that warnings will have meaning. Eight-year-olds need to learn to iron and bake under a watchful (but not critical) eye. Ten-year-olds can begin to have lessons in how to jack up a car safely.

At the 6-year-old level, or even later, many a child causes a great fire hazard by playing with matches. They can hardly—nor should they—be kept out of his way now as they were when he was younger. Telling a child not to play with matches may work very well with one child, for some children are very readily managed or easily impressed. In another child the strength of his desire may be greater than his ability to resist. Even if we wanted to do so, we would hardly think up a punishment that would surely keep every child from experimenting with fire. Children can't possibly have an idea of the danger of such play. We can satisfy their curiosity and give them safe experience by letting them use matches under our guidance and under certain conditions.

WHEN SHOULD A CHILD BE KEPT HOME FROM SCHOOL?

Even though a child shows only slight signs of being under the weather, home is the place for him if he has any of the symptoms listed below.

A running nose, red or running eyes, sneezing or coughing, a rash or a sore throat are signals that tell us a child is coming down with a cold, or with one of the infectious diseases such as measles or whooping cough. And yet where school funds are paid on a basis of average daily attendance children with seemingly slight ailments are not encouraged to stay at home!

A cold or any of the so-called children's diseases is highly contagious during the early stages, so keeping a child at home safeguards both himself and others. If the early symptoms are not neglected, the time a child has to be away from school may be short. If the child turns out to have an infectious disease, rest in bed from the very start may prevent complications which are more serious than the disease itself.

Sometimes symptoms are less noticeable than those given above, but are equally important. Listlessness, tiredness, irritability, or any departure from a child's usual behavior; paleness; a feverish appearance; swelling about the neck, are all causes for keeping a child at home.

Painful symptoms like earache or running ears, vomiting, diarrhea, or headache are so obvious that they can hardly fail to be thought of as good reasons for a child's being put to bed instead of being sent to school. It should be kept in mind that vomiting, often thought of as being due to something a child has eaten, is even more often connected with disease, such as scarlet fever or influenza.

ILLNESS AS AN EXCUSE

Occasionally minor illnesses are made so pleasant by the extra attentions his mother gives—special foods, special toys trotted out for the occasion—that a child pleads sick when he wants to escape something he dreads at school. If there is any suspicion that such an attempt is being made, a child's stay in bed should not be the occasion of a lot of fussing and attention. A few hours will tell whether something is really the matter, or whether he is trying to get his mother's sympathy because he couldn't get any elsewhere. "If you're sick enough to stay at home you're sick enough to be in bed," can be the attitude, and this will give us time to observe whether the illness is real or feigned. A well child seldom wants to stay in bed long if it is not made attractive.

17

The sick child

Parents of school-age children less often have the terrifying experiences with illness that they go through with very young children. No longer is there the helpless panicky feeling that comes when a little child's temperature shoots up alarmingly, but he is able to give only a very vague answer as to where he feels bad.

Too, a mother has learned to know her child and his symptoms by this age period. She knows whether his usual reaction to a cold is severe; she has learned what foods he can take best after a digestive upset; she can often tell by his behavior when it will be better for him to take a good rest in bed than to try to carry on as usual.

It is also easier to get an older child to do the necessary things when he is sick. He can see the reason for taking a lot of fluids, or a disagreeable medicine, and he can also occupy himself more happily during his convalescence, because he can read, and do many things with his hands.

SYMPTOMS OF ILLNESS

It is, of course, just as important to have a doctor's services for a child now as when he was younger, but there will probably be many fewer occasions on which he has to be called. Some of the symptoms when, to be on the safe side, you will want to call your doctor are these:

1. Fever of 102° or above, or persistent temperature over 100°.
2. Vomiting that is severe or occurs over and over.
3. A sore throat.
4. Persistent pain in any part of the body. Earache, severe headache, or pains in the stomach, abdomen, chest, or joints may indicate serious disease, infection, or injury.
5. Stiffness of the neck or back.
6. A breaking out or rash on the child's skin.

BEFORE THE DOCTOR COMES

If you talk to the doctor by phone, tell him as exactly as you can what is wrong, and follow carefully any instructions he gives you.

Until he comes, there are a few things you can do.

1. Put the child to bed in a quiet place where he can rest or fall asleep.
2. Keep other children away from him.
3. If he is vomiting, stop all food but offer water frequently. If he continues to vomit, stop giving even water. After the vomiting subsides, try giving him a few sips of water, ginger ale, or sweetened weak tea. He may have finely cracked ice to suck.
4. If the child is neither vomiting nor having diarrhea, give him liquids—water, fruit juices, milk, or broth—as much as he wishes. *Never try to make a sick child eat.*
5. If he has a high fever and is restless, give him a cool sponge bath to make him more comfortable.
6. Take his temperature every 4 hours and keep a record of it on paper.
7. Save a sample of the child's urine for the doctor.
8. Do not give any medicine unless directed by the doctor.

CARE OF A SICK CHILD

Until the doctor is sure that the child has no communicable disease, keep his handkerchiefs, towels, washcloths, dishes, and toilet utensils separate and sterilize them with boiling water before washing them. Especially boil his handkerchiefs, or, better still, use paper handkerchiefs or tissues which, after use, should be put into a paper bag and burned.

Keep a large apron or a smock in the sick room and wear it while taking care of the child. Before leaving the room, take off the apron and hang it up inside the door. Be sure to change the apron every day.

Wash your hands well with soap and water after caring for the sick child. If the bathroom is not near the sick room, keep a basin of water and a cake of soap on a table just inside the door and wash your hands just before leaving the room.

Avoid spreading disease. One sick person in the family is enough. A sick child, even one who has a simple cold, should be kept in bed.

When a child is acutely ill, and especially when he has a high temperature, he is usually very good about staying in bed. He is drowsy and is likely to sleep off and on most of the time. He prefers not to be disturbed in any way and is not interested in toys or play. During- this period the sick child should not be bothered by any unnecessary attention.

Beyond carrying out the doctor's orders, nothing should be done to him which might be disturbing.

The child who is getting well is, however, a wholly different matter. Many mothers find that keeping a convalescent child in bed is often hard to do. Children have such remarkable powers of recovery that, once over an acute illness, they soon feel fine and begin to clamor to get up before it is safe for them to be out of bed.

A child who has had fever should be kept in bed at least 24 hours after his temperature has reached and stayed normal (98.6° to 99.6°). If he has had fever for more than 2 or 3 days he should stay in bed for 2 or 3 days after his temperature has become normal. If this precaution is always taken, the serious after-effects of many diseases can be avoided.

Cleanliness

Keep a sick child's body clean. Give him a warm sponge bath once or twice a day. Take care that he is not chilled during the bath; he should not be completely uncovered unless the room is warm.

Elimination

If a sick child is not taking much food, his bowels may not move so frequently as usual. If there has been no bowel movement, for 48 hours or if the child seems to have pain in the abdomen, an enema of warm water may be given. (See p. 203.) *Never give a laxative without a doctors advice.* It is sometimes very dangerous to give a laxative, especially if there is pain or swelling of the abdomen.

If the child urinates less frequently than usual, more water should be given to him to drink unless he is vomiting.

A sick child seldom wants to eat or is able to digest as much food as when he is well. In illnesses that do not upset digestion the child may have a simple diet, containing foods such as milk, fruit juices, cereal, egg, toast, vegetables, and simple desserts, unless the doctor orders a special diet.

A sick child needs water, especially if his temperature is high. Water should be offered to him as often as every hour that he is awake. Unless there is a digestive upset, fruit juices also may be given freely. If a child is vomiting, it is sometimes necessary to stop giving water for a time, but it should be started again in small amounts as soon as he can keep it down. Often a child can retain cracked ice or small amounts of ginger ale before he can keep water down.

Taking the temperature

Every mother should learn how to take a child's temperature. It is a good idea to buy a thermometer and learn how to use it when the child is well. Children of 6 and over can have their temperature taken by mouth, but may need reminding not to bite the thermometer.

Before taking the temperature, shake the thermometer down sharply to be sure that the mercury is well below the "normal" mark. Leave it in the child's mouth for 2 minutes by the clock. Write down the degree of temperature and the time of day it was taken.

Colds

A child with a cold should be kept away from other children. A number of contagious diseases besides colds begin with sore throat or a runny nose, and any child with either symptom should be put in a room by himself, away from other children.

Rest in bed is an essential part of the treatment of any cold and will probably hasten the child's recovery.

The coughing accompanying a cold may often be relieved by letting a child breathe air with steam in it. This may be done by placing him in a small room in which water is boiling or a bathroom with hot water running. Doing this several times a day, and just before he goes to bed, may make a child more comfortable.

Do not put nose drops, or anything else, into a child's nose without the advice of a doctor.

If a child's nose is running, a little cold cream or camphor ice smeared under the nose may help to keep the skin from being inflamed.

Teach children to cover the mouth and nose when coughing or sneezing and never to use another person's handkerchief.

Enlarged or diseased tonsils and adenoids

Chronic infection in the tonsils and adenoids is often the cause of colds, sore throats, earaches, running ears, or swollen glands.

Tonsils which are merely enlarged should not be removed if they are not infected and do not interfere with breathing or swallowing. The same holds true for adenoids. Tonsils and adenoids that are frequently or chronically infected, however, need to be removed.

Unless the doctor advises it, do not consider having your child's tonsils or adenoids taken out. Many children never have to have this done.

Sore Throat

Some children, especially the younger ones, may have an inflamed throat without complaining about it. When a throat is inflamed, it is red and may be swollen. White spots or patches in the throat may mean an acute infection of some kind. This may be a simple tonsillitis, or a more serious condition, such as diphtheria or septic sore throat.

Whenever a child has fever or vomits or suddenly refuses food, look at his throat. If it looks inflamed or has patches on it, send for the doctor at once.

Swollen glands

The glands that may become inflamed when children have colds or sore throats are small lumps of tissue just under the jaw on both sides of the neck. They often become swollen when a child has an infection *m* the mouth, nose, throat, or ears. Any swollen glands should be reported to the doctor.

Pneumonia

Pneumonia is a serious disease. It may develop after a cold, measles, whooping cough, or other infection, or it may begin suddenly (primary or acute lobar pneumonia).

The symptoms of pneumonia are fever, cough, and rapid, difficult breathing.

If pneumonia is suspected in a child, a doctor should be called at once. Early treatment with "sulfa" drugs or penicillin in pneumonia *is* truly lifesaving. These drugs, of course, are always given only under your doctor's order.

Laryngitis

If hoarseness in a child lasts more than a few hours he probably has laryngitis—a condition sometimes due to diphtheria. It may accompany or follow a sore throat. A child who has noisy, labored breathing in addition to hoarseness and loss of voice, and seems increasingly sick should be seen by a doctor as soon as possible. Exhaustion and weakness are very serious signs.

If a child has been given diphtheria toxoid when he entered school, or more recently, he will probably have been protected from diphtheria.

Influenza or "grippe"

Epidemic influenza may be very serious in a child, although usually less so than in adults.

The early symptoms of influenza are somewhat like those of a common cold. High fever, vague pains, and marked weakness help to distinguish influenza from a cold.

Pneumonia is the most common and serious complication of influenza. For this reason a child who develops influenza or "grippe" should be seen by a doctor.

Eye disorders

Red or inflamed eyes with watery discharge may be due to inflammation or irritation, to a cinder or dust, or to hay fever.

It is a safe temporary measure for the mother to apply either warm or cold wet compresses in order to relieve swelling and discomfort.

Any speck of dirt that is not washed out soon by the watering of the eye should be removed by a doctor. Any injury of the delicate membranes of the eye is a serious matter.

Discharge of pus from the eyes is a sign of infection, which may be very contagious. Eye infection, if neglected, may lead to permanent injury and blindness. Painful or discharging eyes should be treated by a doctor.

If a child has a squint or if his eyes do not focus properly, a doctor should be consulted with regard to exercise for the eye muscles or other treatment. It has been found recently that, in some cases, operation on eye muscles in early childhood is the best way to remedy these defects.

Eyestrain may show itself by redness of the eyelids, by blinking, or by general irritability. Poor sight may be unnoticed by parents, and some children who are thought to be clumsy or dull in school may have serious eye defects. The possibility of poor vision should be considered if a child has these symptoms.

Sties

A stye or pimple on the edge of the eyelid is caused by an infection entering at the base of an eyelash. The infection is usually introduced by rubbing the eyes, and when a stye forms, the irritation makes a child even more likely to put his hand to his eye. Placing a hot, moist compress on the eye several times a day may help him to keep from rubbing it. Another stye is likely to follow if the infection is spread by rubbing.

Pinkeye

In pinkeye, inflammation makes the eyes look red and runny. It is very contagious, and therefore easily spread among school children. It looks more serious than it is. Moist, hot applications, and sponging the eyes with boric acid solution may help to relieve the irritation. It is highly important for the towels and washcloths used by a child suffering from pinkeye to be kept separate from those in use by other members of the family.

Ear disorders

An earache or a running ear usually develops during a cold or some other illness. Never try to treat a painful or discharging ear without a doctor's advice. Warm, wet compresses or a well-wrapped hotwater bag may relieve the pain.

Deafness, mastoiditis (inflammation of the mastoid bone), or even meningitis may result from neglected ear infections.

Mastoiditis, which used to be common following ear infections, seldom is seen now if such infections are treated with the newer drugs.

Skin diseases

The common skin eruptions of childhood are:

Impetigo contagiosa.—A very contagious skin disease appearing as blisters which become yellow, crusted sores, most often on the face and hands, spreading from one part of the skin to another and from one child to another.

Scabies or *itch.*—A contagious, itching skin eruption occurring on the body and hands and feet, which spreads by contact from one person to another

Ringworm.—A contagious skin eruption, which appears first as a red patch, healing in the center and spreading at the edges. It may itch. It frequently affects the scalp and in time tends to make the hair break off.

Boils and *pimples.*—Small abscesses in the skin. These may be spread by scratching or rubbing, so that often several may appear in succession. Any inflamed place on the skin should be kept clean and should never be picked or squeezed.

Any one of these conditions should be cared for under the direction of a doctor.

Clothing, bedding, towels, and other things that have been used by anyone with a contagious skin eruption should be boiled or thoroughly sunned before being used again, as reinfections often occur through such articles.

Worms

The common worms seen in childhood are roundworms, which are as large as the ordinary earthworm and easy to recognize, and pin-worms, which are white, threadlike, and less than one-half inch long. They may be seen whipping about in a freshly passed stool. Worm medicines must *never* be given without a doctor's advice. If they are powerful enough to kill worms, they may easily harm a child unless given in just the right dose and under the proper conditions.

In getting rid of pinworms, the importance of cleanliness cannot be emphasized too much. Since, even with worm medicine, children can reinfect themselves by scratching, it is absolutely necessary to keep their hands clean and their nails short. At night they should wear cotton pajamas and cotton gloves. To prevent spreading worms to the other children, all clothing and bed clothing of the child who has them should be kept separate and boiled before being washed. It *is* especially important to scrub and sterilize the toilet seat frequently.

Many mothers have the mistaken idea that any child who is nervous, picks at his nose, or grinds his teeth at night has worms. Worms are rarely the cause of such symptoms.

In regions of the country where hookworms are common, if a child shows any symptoms of this disease (paleness, retarded growth, digestive upsets, and itching feet), examinations of his stool should be made. If worms or eggs are found, treatment should be given at once by a physician.

Lice (pediculosis)

Head lice are sometimes found on a child's scalp and hair. The bites of these insects may cause itching. Sores may result, and the glands at the back of the neck may become swollen.

Ten percent DDT powder (in 90 percent inert talc) should be dusted into the hair and scalp, care being taken to keep the powder out of the eyes by protecting them with gauze squares. The entire head should be wrapped in a scarf or clean towel. After several hours, preferably at bedtime, the scarf should be removed. The next morning the hair should be carefully combed with a fine-tooth comb to get rid of the nits and dead lice. On the seventh day following treatment, the hair should be washed with soap and warm water and allowed to dry, after which the DDT powder should be reapplied in the same manner as before. On the fourteenth day the hair should be given a final shampoo. Although two courses of treatment are usually sufficient, it may be necessary to repeat this treatment. Other children or people in the family may reinfect one another, so that all heads should be carefully examined and treated if nits or lice are found. Brushes and combs should be thoroughly cleaned by scrubbing with soap and water and boiling after they are used for treatment. Any hat that has been worn by a child with lice should be sterilized by spraying with 5 percent DDT solution.

Vomiting

Vomiting may be caused by indigestion, by fatigue, or by over-excitement; it may be the sign of some general bodily disturbance or infection; it may be due to some inflammation or stoppage of the digestive tract, or, rarely, to eating some food to which the child *is* sensitive. It may be the first sign of a communicable disease. If a child vomits more than once, he should be put to bed. If he seems sick or feverish or if the vomiting continues, the doctor should be sent for, because the loss of body fluids from persistent vomiting, especially when accompanied by diarrhea, may rapidly reduce a child to a critical condition.

A child who has eaten heavily when he was tired or when he was crying, angry, frightened, or overexcited, may be unable to digest his food and vomiting is the body's way of getting rid of this undigested material. Such vomiting is not serious, for once the stomach is empty, the trouble is usually over.

Occasionally vomiting becomes a habit. This may result from such a condition as whooping cough, or it may start with no obvious cause. Such habitual vomiting is difficult to handle and should, therefore, be treated by a physician.

Constipation

When a child whose bowels are usually regular goes for a day with no movement or with a very small, hard movement, nothing need be done unless he seems sick. He will probably have a large movement the next day.

If a child has pain in the abdomen, nausea, or vomiting and also constipation, this combination of symptoms may point to a serious condition. A small enema may be given but *never* any medicine or laxative of any kind. If relief is not prompt, a doctor should be called at once.

Children who are on a good diet, drink plenty of water, and have good, regular health habits rarely become constipated. Teach your children to report to you if their bowels fail to move for more than 1 day at a time. If constipation occurs often consult your doctor.

Chickenpox   ,

Chickenpox is seldom serious, and complications are rare. It is an entirely different disease from smallpox. It is easily spread by contact with material from a skin eruption or from sores in the nose and mouth of someone with the disease. About 2 weeks pass between contact and appearance of the disease.

The first symptoms may be fever, followed by an eruption within 24 to 36 hours, but often there is no sign of the disease until the rash appears. The rash begins as small red spots, which become small busters—first filled with clear fluid and later with pus. Some children have only two or three spots altogether but usually crops of these come out over a period of 3 to 4 days. As they burst, scabs form. The rash itches, but scratching tends to produce scars and children should be cautioned not to scratch themselves. A paste of baking soda and water will give some relief from the itching. Mitts worn at night may help to keep a child from scratching in his sleep.

Diphtheria

Diphtheria is spread when the discharges from the nose and throat of a person who has the disease or is a carrier of the disease reach the nose or throat of a well person. Sometimes infected throat discharges get into a milk supply; such milk is a source of infection to all who drink it. It takes 2 to 5 days after exposure for the disease to develop. The first symptoms are sore throat, hoarseness, croup, and fever. A grayish membrane may develop in the throat. The fever is usually not high and generally the child looks much sicker than his temperature would indicate. Headache and vomiting may be present.

A doctor should always be called if diphtheria is suspected, because the earlier antitoxin is given, the more effective it is. Diphtheria is a serious disease, and complications are frequent and serious if treatment is delayed.

Diphtheria can be prevented by injections of toxoid in infancy. Children who have been immunized in infancy should have another injection of toxoid when they enter school. The doctor may consider this unnecessary if the Schick test is negative at this time.

Very few persons get diphtheria more than once.

Measles

Measles is not as serious in older children as in younger children. Measles is very contagious. It is spread by discharges from the nose and mouth of an infected person that reach the nose and mouth of the well child. The disease usually develops 10 to 14 days after exposure, although measles has been known to develop in as short a time as 7 days after exposure, or as long as 21 days. Early symptoms are fever, cough, watery eyes, runny nose, and general fatigue. The rash, which is red, irregular, and bumpy, appears 3 to 4 days after the beginning of the symptoms—first around the neck and ears, then on the rest of the body, including the face. Small, bluish spots (Koplik's spots) occur on the inside of the lips and cheeks before the rash appears. The disease can be given to others from the time the first symptoms appear until about a week after the appearance of the rash.

Complications such as ear infection and pneumonia develop in some children after measles. Much can be done to prevent these complications by following the doctor's advice carefully and keeping the child in bed long enough.

If a mother knows that her child has been exposed to measles, she should take him to a doctor.

One attack usually makes the child resistant to later attacks. Some people, however, have measles more than once.

German measles

German, or "3-day," measles is not a serious disease. Complications following it are rare, but it is very contagious.

The rash, which may look like either a measles or a scarlet-fever rash (except that it is usually less red), appears within the first 24 to 36 hours of illness. The rash is often the first, and may be the only, sign of illness. The glands at the base of the skull, however, are generally enlarged.

There is no specific treatment for German measles, but a doctor should see the child to verify the diagnosis.

Mumps

Mumps is not a serious disease. It can, however, have serious complications, which fortunately are rare.

The symptoms of mumps are fever and pain and swelling of the gland (parotid) just below and in front of the ear on one or both sides. There may also be pain on chewing and swallowing.

A doctor should be called to see a child suspected of mumps to decide whether the child has this disease or swollen glands, as the treatment of the two diseases is not the same.

Whooping cough

Whooping cough is a less serious disease in later childhood than in infancy. It is spread by discharges from the throat of a person sick with the disease. Whooping cough begins slowly and gradually. It starts with a cough like the one that accompanies many common colds. This cough usually lasts about 2 weeks before the whooping begins. Whooping cough is contagious during this early period before the appearance of the whoop. Since the diagnosis is difficult during this stage, often the disease is not recognized, and many children spread the infection before it is known that they have it. If there is whooping cough in the neighborhood, a mother should be on the alert for the development of even a slight cough in her child. A school-age child may, if care is not taken, bring home the disease to younger children in the family for whom it is more serious.

If a mother has any reason to suspect that her child has whooping cough she should call the doctor.

Scarlet fever

Scarlet fever may be either mild or quite severe. Whether mild or severe, it is contagious for other children. It is spread by discharges or droplets from the nose and throat of an infected person or carrier. It can also be spread by milk which has been contaminated with the discharge of germs from an infected person or carrier.

The symptoms of scarlet fever appear 2 to 7 days after exposure to the disease. It usually begins suddenly with nausea, vomiting, fever, and sore throat followed by the rash, which generally appears on the second or third day. The rash comes out first on the neck and chest, spreads over the entire body, except the face and scalp, and consists of pin-point red spots on a reddish background.

A doctor should be called at once if a child is suspected of having scarlet fever. The doctor will know how to treat the child to help prevent serious complications. He will also take measures to safeguard the other members of the family and the community from the spread of the disease. "Sulfa" drugs, convalescent serum, and scarlet-fever antitoxin are given in certain cases.

Poliomyelitis (infantile paralysis)

Of the children who get infantile paralysis, or poliomyelitis, only 10 to 50 percent become paralyzed in the acute stage of the disease. Fortunately, the number of those seriously or permanently crippled is small and recovery from paralysis is possible up to a year or so after the attack. Very few persons get infantile paralysis more than once.

Among the early symptoms of the disease are moderate fever, headache, occasional vomiting, drowsiness, and fretfulness. Stiffness or pain in the back or the back of the neck is especially typical. Paralysis, if it occurs, follows a few hours to a few days later. Occasionally paralysis appears without any previous symptoms.

A doctor should be called at once if these symptoms appear and infantile paralysis is suspected. There is no specific treatment for the disease, but proper medical and good nursing care in the early stages are highly important.

Meningitis

Meningitis is a very serious infectious disease. It can be caused by many germs, but the germ that causes most epidemics of so-called spinal meningitis is the meningococcus. The early symptoms of meningitis are abrupt onset of fever, headache, vomiting, and stiffness of the neck. Vomiting tends to be forceful (projectile). Sore throat and a rash may be present.

It is imperative that a doctor be called immediately if a child shows these symptoms, because the earlier treatment is begun the greater the chance for recovery. Not all varieties of meningitis can be cured, but there are new methods of treatment that have made this disease far less to be feared than it once was.

Vaginitis

Vaginal discharge may occur in little girls. It may follow an acute infection or be due to lack of cleanliness. It may, however, also be due to gonococcus infection, which is contagious and is a serious condition. Any child with a vaginal discharge should be examined by a doctor. In particular, the discharge should be examined to determine whether it is the result of a gonococcus infection. If promptly and thoroughly treated, this disease can be completely cured by the newer methods of treatment.

Rheumatic fever

Rheumatic fever is a disease which usually begins in childhood. It most commonly occurs in the school-age child, and tends to come back again and again. The cause of it is not known, but infections with the streptococcus often lead to repeated attacks of rheumatic fever.

The early symptoms of rheumatic fever tend to be like the early symptoms of many other diseases of childhood—loss of appetite, failure to gain weight, rapid pulse, and pain (often vague and fleeting) in joints and muscles. Pain and swelling of first one joint and then another, usually with high fever, are more definite signs of rheumatic infection.

Chorea, popularly known as St. Vitus' dance, is another form of rheumatic fever. Awkward, jerky movements of the face, arms, and legs—noticeable when the child tries to feed himself, dress himself, or pick up objects—and unexplained crying spells are symptoms that may mean the child has chorea.

If a child develops symptoms which suggest rheumatic fever, a doctor should be consulted at once.

After an attack of rheumatic fever a child may be left with some scarring of the heart, which is known as rheumatic heart disease. Rheumatic heart disease does not usually prevent a child from leading a normal life, provided the period of rest in bed is strictly adhered to while he is recovering from an attack.

Contrary to a rather widespread belief, children with rheumatic heart disease do not "drop dead." This mistaken idea has arisen from a popular confusion between heart disease of the rheumatic type in children and heart disease of an entirely different nature in adults.

It is important to find out whether a child has rheumatic heart disease, because if he has, he is likely to have another attack of rheumatic fever, and measures should be taken to prevent this. The diagnosis of rheumatic heart disease cannot usually be made by physical examination alone, since a large number of perfectly normal children have "heart murmurs." In order to decide whether a murmur indicates heart disease or not, the doctor will want a complete medical history, a complete physical examination, and laboratory examinations, such as X-ray, fluoroscopic examinations, and electrocardiogram.

Tuberculosis

Tuberculosis in childhood may affect almost any part of the body. It may affect the lungs, but it most commonly affects the glands—especially those inside the chest and abdomen—and the joints and bones. Tuberculosis may also cause inflammation of the lining of the chest (pleurisy), the covering of the brain (meningitis), the lining of the abdomen (peritonitis), the membranes of the eye (conjunctivitis), and the skin.

Tuberculosis is acquired most often by contact with someone who has it, by drinking raw milk from tuberculous cows, or by eating milk products made from such raw milk.

Some of the symptoms common to all types of tuberculosis are: Loss in weight or failure to gain weight, unexplained fever, enlarged glands, pallor, and fatigue. Unlike adults, children with tuberculosis rarely have a cough as a symptom.

A child should never live in the same household with anyone who has tuberculosis. All children who have come in contact with such a person should be examined by a doctor and have a tuberculin test. Those with positive tuberculin reactions should also have an X-ray of the chest; those with negative reactions should have the test repeated periodically.

Young children who get tuberculosis have a good chance for recovery, provided the diagnosis of the disease is made early. For this reason, if a child has any of the symptoms of tuberculosis listed or if he has been in contact with a person known or suspected to have tuberculosis, he should be taken to a doctor at once for thorough examination, X-rays, and testing.

Anemia

Anemia is a condition in which the child's blood has less red coloring matter than it has under normal conditions. If a child habitually looks pale, the doctor should be consulted; he will probably make a test of the blood to find out whether the child has anemia. There are several reasons why a child may have anemia.

1. He may have had a severe illness in which some of his blood was used up. A general building up after the illness will cure this type of anemia.

2. He may have had a wound that bled a great deal. If the loss has been very great, it may be necessary to give him a transfusion of someone else's blood. If the loss has not been too great, he will recover from the anemia without a transfusion.

Asthma, hay fever, and hives

Some children when exposed to substances to which they are sensitive develop symptoms like asthma, hay fever, or hives.

Asthma is a condition in which the child has such difficulty in breathing that he wheezes. Asthma may be very mild, but sometimes it is so severe that the child is unable to lie down and must sleep propped up or in a chair. There is usually a severe cough with an asthmatic attack, but unless infection is present also, there is seldom any fever. Asthma may result from eating some food to which the child is sensitive, as egg, or it may result from contact with some fine substance which he breathes in, as house dust, feathers, or animal hair. Sometimes asthma is associated with colds or other infections.

Hay fever is characterized by sneezing, itching eyes, and swelling of the membranes of the nose. It can be produced by any of the substances which cause asthma but is more commonly caused by pollen of weeds and grasses.

Hives are itching, raised areas on the skin which look like large mosquito bites. They come out suddenly and often disappear quickly and are most commonly due to some food to which the child is sensitive.

A child with any form of chronic allergy (sensitiveness to certain foods, pollens, and so forth) should be under the care of a physician, who by means of tests, trial diets, or changes in the home, will try to find out what the child is sensitive to. Each case is different and needs to be treated individually. In some cases it is not difficult to find the offending substance and remove it so that he has complete relief. In other cases the child is sensitive to so many things that the particular offenders cannot be found. If the child has severe and repeated attacks, it may be worth while to go to great effort to find and remove the cause. If it is necessary to deprive a child of any article of food over a considerable length of time, however, a satisfactory substitute should be found. No child should be deprived of the essential foods for growth. It should be remembered that allergic conditions are seldom fatal and that many children outgrow them.

Children who have received sera (usually horse serum) for treatment or prevention of disease may become sensitive to substances in them so that if they are given the same kind of serum again they develop symptoms of asthma, hay fever, or hives. If it is necessary for your child to receive a serum, *do not forget to tell the doctor about any injection that he has had before.* The usual materials used for injection to prevent diphtheria and whooping cough do not contain horse serum.

In some cases, the question arises as to whether a change of climate may not benefit, other methods of treatment having failed.

The United States Public Health Service makes several suggestions to those contemplating such a move. First, keep in mind that "no two cases of asthma are exactly alike," and that a location that has ben-fitted someone else may not in the present case give relief.

Second, "don't make a drastic change of location for asthma without the guidance of your physician, and, if possible, one or more specialists."

Third, "make any change of climate on a trial basis for a year or two. Although most people suffering from asthma and sinusitis react well to the dry, warm climate of the Southwest, some get worse in the very dry air."

Twitching and other habit spasms

Twitching of the face, blinking of the eyes, making faces, and other odd repeated movements are called habit spasms or tics. They may be signs of general fatigue or, occasionally, of some physical irritation, but more frequently they indicate the inability of the child to adjust himself to some emotional or nervous strain of which neither child nor parent is aware. Stuttering and stammering are habit spasms, occasionally due to imitation but usually to some nervous strain. When a child shows symptoms of this type, he should be taken to a doctor. If the underlying cause is to be found, it is important to discuss with the doctor the problems of the family life as well as the child's routine.

Kidney disease

Kidney disease in children may take several forms. The two most common of these are acute nephritis and pyelitis.

Acute nephritis is an inflammation of the kidneys, which may follow a sore throat, scarlet fever, or other infection. Occasionally, however, acute nephritis may appear in a child who previously has seemed well. The urine is usually scanty and dark-colored and it may be slightly or even quite bloody. The child may not seem very sick; but as the disease can be serious, a doctor should be called if a child shows these symptoms.

Pyelitis is an infection of the kidneys in which pus is present in the urine. The symptoms of this disease are often vague. The child may have fever or headache and seem sick but complain of no pain, or he may have to urinate frequently and complain of pain on urination. Pyelitis is more common among girls.

Since neither of these diseases can be diagnosed without examination of the child's urine, the mother should always save a sample for the doctor whenever a child is sick.

The doctor may try sulfa drugs or streptomycin in treating these diseases, as they have been of benefit in many cases.

Diabetes mellitus

Children, as well as adults, may suffer from diabetes mellitus. With this disease the body is unable to use the sugars and starches of the diet, and sugar is excreted in the urine. Formerly it was almost always fatal in childhood. Now with the use of insulin and diets carefully prescribed by a doctor, the disease may be so controlled that a child can continue to grow and live a normal and happy life.

If a child begins to drink unusually large amounts of water, urinates freely in very large amounts, or has a very hearty appetite and yet loses weight, take him to the doctor at once, as these may be the early symptoms of diabetes. Carry a specimen of urine with you for examination.

Appendicitis

If appendicitis is diagnosed promptly and operation is performed early, complete recovery is the rule. It is only when the condition is not diagnosed early enough and operation is delayed that appendicitis becomes dangerous.

The early symptoms of appendicitis are nausea, fever, which may be only slight, pain in the abdomen, and sometimes vomiting. The pain may seem to be in the region of the stomach or it may be in the right side (rarely the left side). A child with these symptoms should be seen by a doctor immediately. Any child with persistent abdominal pain which lasts more than a short time, even in the absence of other symptoms, should be seen by a doctor. A *laxative should never be given to a child with abdominal pains.*

ACCIDENTS

All but very minor cuts, burns, and other injuries should be treated by a doctor, in the home, office, or hospital. If you have taken a course in first aid, put into practice what you have been taught. Remember, however, that first aid is only *first* aid. In all but very slight injuries or minor accidents, have your child seen by a doctor at the earliest possible moment.

CUTS

Do

1. If small, wash out well with soap and water and apply sterile bandage, or clean, freshly ironed piece of cloth.

2. If large, cover with sterile gauze, press gauze firmly over wound to control bleeding, and hold in place until the doctor comes.

Don't

1. If small, don't use strong antiseptics. Fresh tincture of iodine (half strength) or alcohol may be used if desired. Soap and water is an excellent antiseptic.

2. If large, don't do anything except cover with sterile gauze, control bleeding, and let the doctor do the rest.

PUNCTURE WOUNDS

1. If not bleeding freely, try to encourage bleeding by pressing again and again just above wound, and, in the case of a finger or toe, by squeezing or "milking" it.

2. Be sure to ask the doctor in every case if he thinks tetanus antitoxin advisable.

Don't

1. Don't ever try to close a puncture wound with bandage, adhesive, or anything else. A sterile gauze pad may be placed loosely over wound until the doctor comes.

2. Don't forget to tell the doctor if your child has had any kind of serum before.

BLEEDING

Do

1. If from a blood vessel in the arm or leg, apply pressure to the proper pressure point. If pressure points are not: known, apply a tight band or tourniquet to the upper arm or upper leg, as the case may be. Get the doctor immediately.

2. If from some other part of the body, place thick sterile gauze pad or clean towel over bleeding point and apply strong pressure. Get the doctor immediately.

Don't

1. Never leave a tourniquet or band in place longer than 15 minutes at a time. After 15 minutes, remove for 2 minutes and then replace tourniquet, if necessary.

BURNS

Do

1. If mild, apply simple non-oily burn ointment or paste made of baking soda and water on a clean, freshly ironed cloth.

2. If severe and widespread, wrap child in clean sheet first, then blankets, and take to hospital or doctor.

Don't

1. Don't use oil or oily substances on any bum. Do not use ab sorbent cotton.

2. Never underestimate a burn. Especially never underestimate sunburn.

BROKEN LIMBS

Do

1. To prevent movement of the part apply a home-made splint. The simplest method is to splint the part with a⁻ pillow. To apply, slide a large pillow under the limb, making sure that pillow is long enough to include the joint at each end of the broken bone. Then fold sides of pillow up over limb and make firm by tying strips of cloth or bandage around the pillow at 3- to 4-inch intervals.

2. If bone fragment has broken through skin, cover bone and wound with sterile gauze dressing. Apply pillow splint and take the child to the doctor immediately.

Don't

1. Don't let child walk on leg or use arm if fracture is suspected.

2. Never apply a splint or bandage tightly. To allow for swelling of the part, provide plenty of padding between limb and splint.

3. Never try to "set" a compound fracture (one in which bone is exposed) and do not apply antiseptics or try to do anything to the wound. Simply cover it with a sterile dressing and let the doctor do the rest.

POISONING

Do
1. Bring about repeated vomiting by giving large amounts of warm antidote.
2. If vomiting does not occur after 3 to 4 glassfuls of soapsuds have been taken, cause vomiting by tickling the back of throat with finger. Then give more soapsuds and do the same thing again. Keep on until the fluid that is vomited is as clean as it was when swallowed. Get the child to hospital or doctor immediately.

Don't
1. Above all, don't lose your head.
2. Never waste precious time trying to look up the proper antidote for a particular poison. If you can bring about vomiting quickly, you will greatly reduce the danger. The doctor will give the proper antidote.

DOG BITE

Do
1. Hold the wound under running water and wash it thoroughly. Dry it with clean gauze and cover it with gauze dressing. Since the doctor will probably want to cauterize the wound, do not use antiseptics before he arrives. The doctor will decide whether or not Pasteur treatment is to be given.

Don't
1. Don't let a well-meaning person shoot the dog. The dog should be caught and kept under observation, to find out whether or not it has rabies.

NOSEBLEED

Do
1. Apply cold, wet cloths over the child's nose and the back of his neck. If this is not effective, pack his nostrils with strips of gauze or bandage, being sure that at least an inch of the pack is left hanging outside the nose. If bleeding still continues, call a doctor.

Don't
1. Never put a child's head in such a position that the blood will back up and go down his throat and thus not be seen.

index

215

Also available from www.sunvillagepublications.com

How To Teach Children
The Joy of Reading

A Guide for Parents and Teachers

Ellen C. Henderson

Launching Your Preschooler

How To Help Make Your Child's
First Experiences A Breeze!

Edgar S. Bley

HOW TO PREVENT STUTTERING IN CHILDREN

A Guide for Parents and Teachers

Leon Lassers, Ph.D.

Teach Your Child To Talk

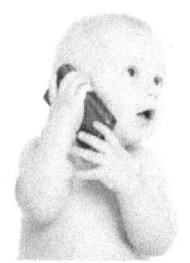

How To Tell Children About Sex

Clyde M. Narramore, Ed.D.